D0936387

A Source Book of Military Tracked Vehicles

Italian design (Pavesi) of 1915

Modern battle tank 'Leopard'

A Source Book of

Military Tracked Vehicles

Compiled by the Olyslager Organization
Edited by Bart H. Vanderveen

WARD LOCK LIMITED · LONDON

Space limitations have necessitated the condensing of the technical data so that in ENGINE it runs: name of engine, number of cylinders (ie 6-in-line), and lastly the type of cooling. Details of the steering system and the vehicle's maximum speed (where known) are included under TRANSMISSION and the number of crew (where applicable) under ARMS. All DIMENSIONS run length × width × height.

ISBN 0 7063 1469 7

First published in Great Britain 1973
by Ward Lock Limited,
116 Baker Street, London, W1M 2BB

Designed by Conal A. Buck

Filmset and printed in England by
Cox and Wyman Ltd,
London, Fakenham and Reading

Foreword

In *A Source Book of Military Wheeled Vehicles* we presented a selection of old and new military vehicles which run on wheels and with the engine power usually applied to more than one axle. In this Source Book, we review a variety of vehicles which are, or were, 'track-laying'. Like wheeled vehicles, these come in various forms and include several half- or semi-track types, i.e. vehicles with tracks for propulsion and ordinary wheels for steering.

Military vehicle enthusiasts have tended to take a greater interest in full-track AFVs (armoured fighting vehicles) than in 'soft skins' probably because the former are more impressive and different from civilian vehicles. These enthusiasts are often those with purely academic, scale-modelling or wargaming interests. For the practical enthusiasts – the collector of the real thing – they present much greater problems than wheeled vehicles. The main drawbacks are, in most cases, the heavy consumption of expensive fuel and taking the vehicle on the road. 'Owning a real tank' is many an enthusiast's dream but so far only few have achieved this goal. There are, of course, light tracked vehicles which are more manageable, such as British and Canadian Universal, Bren Carriers and the American 'Weasel', as well as the half-track types produced by the Americans and Germans in World War II, several of which are now in private collections.

The majority of preserved full-track military vehicles, however, are in military museums, the best of which is undoubtedly the Royal Armoured Corps Tank Museum at Bovington Camp, Dorset, England, where a truly amazing selection has been amassed. It includes specimens of many of the types shown in this book.

Piet Olyslager MSIA, MSAE, KIVI

Fowler 'Steeplechaser' of 1884 had 12 ft hind wheels for maximum ground contact area

Introduction

The 'invention' of the wheel has dramatically changed civilization and today it is difficult to comprehend why it was not discovered even earlier than it was. Of course, the basic wheel has always existed, in the form of the tree trunk. It only needed an inventive mind to slice it up into discs and fit the discs/wheels on to an axle shaft.

The big problem with the ordinary wheel is that, if it is to be of manageable size, it is only suitable for metalled roads and hard surfaces. In soft ground, mud or snow it will sink and to prevent this, it must be made much larger in width and/or diameter. This was, in fact, done on a number of off-road vehicles but their sheer size precluded their use except for special purposes and on locations where size was no problem. David Best in the USA built a 20-ton tractor in 1900 which had wood-covered drive wheels 15 feet wide and 9 feet in diameter.

When normal wheels do sink too deep, we try to minimize the effect by placing mats, planks or something similar in front of and under them so that the weight resting on the wheel (and pushing it down) is spread over a larger area; hence the larger wheels, mentioned earlier, which do exert less pressure per square inch because of their larger ground contact area. This was well-known to our ancestors and at least one of them went so far as to attach flat boards loosely (called *Porte Rails*, portable rails) to the wheel rims in such a way that, as the wheel revolved, the boards were laid down in turn to take the vehicle's weight. This system always remained a clumsy contrivance. Experiments were also carried out with a kind of artificial 'elephant's-foot' attached to the perimeter of the wheel to prevent the wheels from sinking into soft ground.

The portable rail was the ancestor of the endless track in that it automatically laid a track in front of the wheels. On the track-laying vehicles which followed, the chain of boards (links) was made into a separate and longer endless track with two or more wheels running within and on them. Such a device became known as a track bogie.

The firm of R. Hornsby Sons Ltd of Grantham, Lincolnshire, produced their first (if not the first) full-chain-track tractor in 1906–7. It was a converted car with wooden-spoke wheels running within a timber-shod endless chain. The British Army Service Corps at that time had a Hornsby internal-combustion (as opposed to steam) tractor with Ackroyd paraffin engine and had this machine converted to have Hornsby caterpillar tracks in 1907. This machine, Caterpillar No. 1, weighed 23 tons and was steered by track-brakes which were actuated by compressed air. The air was pumped up by means of a handwheel and crank arrangement to 80 lbs per sq in. It was followed in 1909 by what became known as the Little Caterpillar, a tracked tractor which weighed less than half as much and was powered by a 60-bhp high-speed paraffin engine. It had a different type of track, featuring large links, each shod with two rubber or wooden blocks. It was later modified to run on petrol, boosting the horsepower up to 120. The first tractor was scrapped at the outbreak of World War I, but the Little Caterpillar, now fitted with an AEC engine, was kept and still exists today in the RAC Tank Museum at Bovington.

Interest in tracked vehicles in Britain was minimal before World War I. In the United States, however, the Holt Manufacturing Co. developed track units to replace the rear wheels of their agricultural tractors. Holt steam traction engine No. 77 was the first to be tested with rear track bogies, on 24 November 1904. Each bogie was 30 inches high, 42 inches wide and 9 feet long. The tracks consisted of 3×4-inch wooden slats. It was estimated that these track bogies had as much bearing surface as 75-feet diameter wheels! Many thousands of these semi-track Holt Caterpillars were subsequently made. The Caterpillar name was registered by Holt as a trade name in 1910 and when the Holt company merged with the C. L. Best Tractor Co. (another pioneering firm) in 1925, the new corporate name chosen was Caterpillar Tractor Company. Meanwhile, in

Boydell/Burrell traction engine with *Porte Rails,* progenitors of the chain tracks. c. 1856

November 1912, Hornsby sold their American and Canadian patents to the Holt Mfg Co. of Stockton, California and the Holt Caterpillar Co. of New York, for the sum of £4,000!

Once the pattern was set, subsequent progress was rapid. World War I, as we all know, saw the birth of the tank, i.e. the full-track armoured fighting vehicle which was able to negotiate the roughest shell-torn grounds of the French and Flanders battlefields.

Again, the idea for a practical application originated in Britain. Designs for tracked fighting vehicles had been in existence for some time, mainly on drawing boards but also in prototype form. One of the main problems with full-tracked vehicles was steering them. Many of the early machines had one or two ordinary wheels at the front or rear for steering purposes, while track brakes or steering clutches were applied for acute turns. Gradually the steering systems became more refined but only at the cost of sometimes appalling complexity.

Hornsby/Ackroyd 'Caterpillar No. 1' of 1907

It is interesting to cast our minds back to the earliest days of the tank; a name, incidentally, which was used for security reasons, the first machines being labelled as 'water tanks' for shipment to Petrograd, Russia. The surprise element was most effective. Work on the early tanks, then known as 'landships' was done by the Admiralty Landship Committee, set up in February 1915. They studied and tested several American semi-track machines and designed some full-track types in conjunction with William Foster & Co Ltd of Lincoln. From these early machines (Little Willie and Mother) evolved the British heavy tanks of World War I.

At the end of August 1916, the first two companies of what later became the Tank Corps (then called the Heavy Branch, Machine Gun Corps for purposes of secrecy) were sent to France with 50 tanks. They first used these in mid-September, on the Somme Front. Their effect, both on the British and German troops, was electrical. They were painted in what naturalists call protective colours:

British heavy tanks being examined and tested by the Germans after capture in 1916–17

browns, yellows and greens, and appeared like snakes or lizards, harmonizing with the desolated environment in which they moved. They were indeed a terrifying sight to those who watched them first, on that morning of 15 September, dimly outlined in the grey light of dawn, spitting fire and death over the shell-torn ground and trenches. Their first action was not very successful, however, mainly due to improper planning. But an air pilot's wireless said: 'A tank is walking up the high street,

German Bremer 'Marienwagen', four-track conversion of a Daimler 4 ton truck. 1916

with the British Army cheering behind it.' This was an actual fact. One of the motorized monsters was there, down below him, enjoying itself thoroughly in keeping down the heads of the enemy. It had a big notice on it, saying 'Great Hun Defeat, Special!'

It was something completely new on the battlefield. Poison gas was known to antiquity, the first submarine had been invented by Fulton over 100 years previously and the aeroplane was soaring high when war engulfed Europe in 1914. The substitution of the armoured, moving, firing line for the unarmoured static firing line constituted a revolution in tactics which was probably the greatest ever made. At the battle of Cambrai in November 1917, 378 tanks broke through the Hindenburg Line to a depth of 10,000 yards. At Ypres the British had used 120,000 gunners and fired, in the preliminary bombardment alone, 4,280,000 shells weighing 120,000 tons and costing £22,200,000; yet it took over three months to penetrate to a depth of 10,000 yards and this

Swedish Landsverk 5 wheel-cum-track chassis; wheels could be lowered for high-speed operation on paved roads. 1929

German NSU semi-track with motorcycle front end for normal steering, track brakes for tight turns. 1941

Typical US SP Artillery: M107 175 mm gun and (behind) M109 155 mm howitzer. 1960s

War-surplus 'Sherman' tank used as SP carriage for multi-bucket conveyor in the Soviet Union

penetration cost 400,000 casualties. At Cambrai only 4,000 tank men were used; there was no preliminary bombardment and it took only twelve hours to penetrate 10,000 yards. The number of casualties was about 5,000. In August 1918 at Amiens, which was the greatest tank battle of the war, the battle which Ludendorff christened 'the black day of the German Army', the Allied casualties amounted to slightly under 1,000. Thus, the tank proved itself not only a victory-winner but also a life-saver.

The rest of the tank story is complex and one of continuous improvements, both from an automotive and a military tactical point of view. Rapid progress in technology enabled designers and manufacturers to produce increasingly sophisticated vehicles with very high performance and gun power. The mechanical components of most of the successful tanks have been and are used as well for special purpose vehicles such as armoured recovery vehicles (ARVs), bridge layers, self-propelled artillery (SPs) and other types, as will be seen in the following pages which portray some of the thousands of tracked vehicles used by the world's armed forces since those 'terrifying monsters' of September 1916.

The designers' dilemma, wheels or tracks, for light and medium AFVs and tractors still exists. Most of these vehicles are used on the roads as well as off them. On the roads, the wheeled vehicle is faster, quieter and easier to drive. Off the beaten track however, the tracked vehicle is superior. In the past there have been compromise solutions like the semi-track, the four-track and the wheel-cum-track, and even tanks which could run without their tracks. None of these were very successful and both the wheeled and the tracked vehicle have now been developed to an extent whereby, particularly for vehicles like armoured personnel carriers, it is extremely difficult for the customer to decide what to choose. At least one vehicle, the French AMX10, was produced with tracks (AMX70P) but with a choice of wheels (AMX10R) as well.

Glossary

This Source Book presents a random selection of full- and semi-tracked military motor vehicles as used from World War I up to the present day. The accent is on World War II, when the number of types used by the various belligerent powers was colossal. Vehicles of this period also tend to be the most popular in terms of interest shown by enthusiasts.

Because of the often long production and service spans of AFVs, no attempt has been made to follow a strictly chronological order. This was also impractical because in peacetime there is usually a very long development period between the first prototype and the moment when the vehicle enters service. Therefore we have used the following division of periods:

1. World War I
2. the 1920s
3. the 1930s
4. World War II
5. the 1950s
6. the 1960s
7. the 1970s.

Even this division is sometimes difficult to apply but the period stated is the one during which the vehicles saw most of their initial service. World War II vehicles, in particular, remained in use for a long time afterwards, although often modified or modernized. Some are still in use today. Within the period, the sub-divisions or sequences are as follows:

1. tractors (all types)
2. amphibians
3. carriers (APCs, etc.)
4. tanks (light, medium, cruiser, infantry, heavy)
5. self-propelled artillery (SPs of all types)
6. special vehicles (bridging, mine-clearing, etc.)
7. miscellaneous vehicles (bulldozers, half-track trucks, etc.) In each sub-division, vehicles are shown in alphabetical order of the country of origin.

The brief technical data has been extracted from a variety of sources but many details, especially dimensions, must be considered as approximate since even official publications are often contradictory. Weights and dimensions are given in the units which are generally used in the country where the vehicle was manufactured.

Abbreviations

AFV	armoured fighting vehicle
APC	armoured personnel carrier
ARV	armoured recovery vehicle
bhp	brake horsepower
CID	cubic inches displacement
F.R	number of speeds forward and reverse
OHV	overhead valve
pdr	pounder (for guns)
shp	shaft horsepower
SP	self-propelled

WW I Holt (USA)
Caterpillar 75

Produced in large numbers by the Holt Manufacturing Co. of Stockton, California, for several governments throughout World War I. It was also built in Britain (Ruston). Basically an agricultural tractor, the military used it to haul heavy artillery. A 6-cylinder 120 bhp version was also produced.
Type: Artillery tractor.
Engine: Holt 75, 4-in-line cyl., 75 bhp at 550 rpm (50 drawbar hp). Liquid cooling.
Transmission: 2 F 1 R, steering by front wheel and drive shaft steering clutches. 3 mph.
Crew: 2
Dimensions: 240 in long × 116 in wide × 120 in high. 24,000 lbs approx.

WW I Holt (USA)

Caterpillar G9

In 1917 the Holt Manufacturing Co. produced this experimental armoured vehicle, based on the Holt 75 half-track tractor. It was designated G9 and had two turrets, namely a large one at the rear (shown) and a smaller one in front. It was tested by the US Army Ordnance Dept. but remained at prototype stage, like other Holt designs with steam and petrol-electric propulsion.

Type: Experimental tank.

WW I (USA)

10 ton M1917

Used for towing 155 mm GPF gun (shown), or 9.2 in howitzer or 10 ton trailer. Designed in 1917, just over 2,000 had been delivered by the end of January 1919. There were also 2½ and 5 ton models, built by various manufacturers to common military designs. After the war many were turned over to US state highway departments.

Type: Artillery tractor.
Engine: OHV, 922CID, 4-in-line cyl., 67 bhp at 600 rpm. Liquid cooling.
Transmission: 3 F 1 R gearbox (direct drive or second speed), dry-plate multiple-disc type steering clutches. 6.5 mph.
Crew: 3
Dimensions: 162 in × 76 in. 21,500 lbs approx.

WW I Renault (F)
FT17

One of the world's first and most successful tanks which remained in use until and including World War II. Conceived by General Estienne in 1916 and designed by Louis Renault, several thousands were built by Renault and three co-producers. After World War I many were sold to other countries. There were several variants, including even a bulldozer and a bridge-layer. Armour was 6.22 mm thick.

Type: Light tank.
Engine: Renault 4.48 litre, 4-in-line cyl., 35 bhp. Liquid cooling.
Transmission: 4 F 1 R, track brake steering. 8 kph.
Arms: 37 mm gun or 75 mm gun or 1 machine gun. 2 crew.
Dimensions: 4.04 m × 1.74 m × 2.14 m. 6½ tons approx.

WW I Ford (USA)

3 ton

It was designed originally as a machine gun or ammunition carrier and employed many components of Ford's legendary Model T car. The Ford Motor Co. were to produce over 15,000 units but after 15 had been built, the Armistice came and orders were cancelled. Note the large front wheels. Armour was $\frac{1}{4}$–$\frac{1}{2}$ in thick.

Type: Light tank.

Engine: 2 Ford T, 4-in-line, 45 bhp each. Liquid.

Transmission: Planetary type 2 F 1 R gearboxes for each track, clutch brake steering. 8 mph.

Arms: 1 machine gun. Crew 2.

Dimensions: 165 in×66 in×63 in. 6,800 lbs approx.

WW I Ford (USA)

3 man

It was designed as a heavier, more powerful version of the Ford 3-ton tank with more gunpower. The Ford T engines were replaced by one Hudson power unit but the earlier transmission system was retained. Orders were cancelled in 1919. Armour was 0.37–0.5 in thick.

Type: Light tank.

Engine: Hudson Six, 6-in-line, 60 bhp. Liquid.

Transmission: Planetary type 2 F 1 R gearboxes for each track, clutch steering. 9 mph.

Arms: 37 mm gun, 1 machine gun. 3 crew.

Dimensions: 198 in×78 in×93 in. 15,000 lbs approx.

WW I Pioneer Tractor Co. (USA)

8 ton, Skeleton

The 'Skeleton Tank' was a product of the Pioneer Tractor Company of Stillwater and Winona in Minnesota. It was constructed from iron pipes, forming a lozenge shape. This is a $\frac{3}{4}$-front view. It was designed in 1918 to be capable of crossing wide trenches.
Type: Light tank.
Engine: 2 Beaver Four, 4-in-line, 50 bhp each. Liquid.
Transmission: 2 F 1 R, shaft drive to rear sprockets. 8 mph.
Arms: 1 machine gun. 2 crew.
Dimensions: 300 in × 101 in × 114 in. 16,000 lbs approx.

WW I (F)

St Chamond

This large machine was introduced in 1916 and first saw action in May 1917. Some were supplied to Russia after the 1917 revolution and following capture, saw service with the Red Army. Gun-less vehicles were employed as supply carriers.
Type: Medium tank.
Engine: Panhard (sleeve-valve), 4-in-line, 90 bhp at 1,350 rpm. Liquid.
Transmission: Petrol-electric, steering by speed variations of electric motors driving each track. 8.5 kph.
Arms: 75 mm gun, 4 machine guns. 9 crew.
Dimensions: 7.91 m × 2.67 m × 2.36 m. 23,000 kg approx.

WW I W. Foster & Co. (GB)

Mk A, 'Whippet'

From October 1917, 200 were produced by William Foster & Co. of Lincoln. Intended for fast cavalry and pursuit work. Also known as the 'Tritton Chaser'. Shown here launching a fishing boat in France.
Type: Medium tank.
Engine: 2 Tylor JB, 4-in-line, 45 bhp each. Liquid.

Transmission: 4 F 1 R, each engine driving one track. Steered by varying an engine speed and steering-wheel. 8 mph.
Arms: 3 Hotchkiss machine guns. 3 crew.
Dimensions: 20 ft×8 ft 7 in×9 ft. 14 tons approx.

WW I (D)
Sturmpanzerwagen A7V

This was the only operational German tank (of their own manufacture) of World War I. It was named after *Allgemeine Kriegsdepartment 7. Abteilung für Verkehrswesen*, which was the committee responsible for the vehicle's design and production. In addition to just over 20 A7V tanks, some 75 unarmoured supply carriers were built using the same undercarriage.

Type: Heavy tank.
Engine: 2 Daimler 165204, 17 litre, 4-in-line, 100 bhp at 900 rpm. Liquid.
Transmission: 3F3R, steering by throttle control assisted by clutches and track brakes. 12 kph.
Arms: 5.7 cm gun in nose and 6–7 machine guns. 18 crew.
Dimensions: 7.35 m × 3.10 m × 3.40 m. 32,000 kg approx.

WW I (GB)
Heavy Tank, Mks I–III

Built in 1916–17 these were the first tanks, or 'landships', to go into action in France in August 1917. Three of the crew members did the steering and gear shifting, in accordance with hand signals given by the driver. Heavy and cumbersome, these first tanks nevertheless created a breakthrough in warfare and they soon developed into more manageable machines.
Type: Heavy tank.
Engine: Daimler-Foster, 6-in-line, 105 bhp. Liquid.
Transmission: 2 F 1 R with 2-speed auxiliary gearboxes for each track. (Locked for straight-ahead). 3–4 mph.
Arms: 'Male' versions had guns and machine guns, 'Female' only machine guns, all in sponsons on the sides of the hull. 8 crew.
Dimensions: 26 ft 5 in × 14 ft × 8 ft 2 in. 27–8 tons.

WW I (F)
Schneider CD

This 3 ton gun portee was based on the chassis of the Schneider CA medium tank and was used to transport the 155 mm gun M1917. It was produced in 1917. Renault also produced a *Caterpillar Porteur* (an 8 ton model with 110 bhp engine).
Type: Artillery carrier.
Engine: Schneider Special, 4-in-line, 60 bhp at 1,000 rpm. Liquid.
Transmission: 3 F 1 R, steering by differential brakes. 8 kph.
Crew: 1.
Dimensions: 5 m × 2 m × 2.5 m approx. 10,000 kg approx.

WW I (GB)
Mk III 'Light Dragon'

It was based on the Vickers Mk II medium tank of 1927. It superseded the 'Light Dragons' Mk I of 1922 and Mk II of 1925. Its towing capacity was 15 tons.
Type: Artillery tractor.
Engine: Armstrong-Siddeley V8, 8-in-V, 90 bhp at 1,750 rpm. Air.
Transmission: 4-speed gearbox and 2-speed planetary transmission, clutch and brake steering. 22 mph.
Crew: 2.
Dimensions: 17 ft 5 in × 9 ft approx. 8 tons.

1920s Fiat (I)
3000 Mod. 21

An Italian-produced version of the French Renault FT light tank (q.v.), but not used in World War I. Prototypes, featuring transversally-mounted Fiat engine, developed during 1920–1. Production models entered service in 1923. Improved Model 30 had more power and a 37 mm gun.
Type: Light tank.
Engine: Fiat 6.2 litre, 4-in-line, 50 bhp at 1,700 rpm. Liquid.
Transmission: 3 F 1 R, track brake steering. 20 kph.
Arms: 2 machine guns. 2 crew.
Dimensions: 4.17 m × 1.64 m × 2.19 m. 5,500 kg approx.

See following page

1920s (USA)
Convertible M1928

Built in 1928 by the US Wheel Track Layer Corp. to the design of Walter Christie, one of the world's best known tank designers. It could run on either wheels or tracks. It is shown during a demonstration at the Capitol in Washington D.C., in 1930. It developed into the Christie medium tanks T3, etc.
Type: Medium tank.
Engine: Liberty V12, 12-in-V, 338 bhp. Liquid.
Transmission: 4 F 1 R, on road the road wheels were chain-driven from the main driving wheels. 70 mph, 42 mph on tracks.
Arms: Mock-up gun in nose, pedestal for machine gun in front compartment. 3 crew.
Dimensions: 204 in × 84 in × 72 in. 17,200 lbs approx.

1920s FCM (F)
2C

These heavy and large twin-turret tanks were produced by the *Société des Forges et Chautiers de Mediterranée* (FCM) but no more than ten had been delivered by the time of the Armistice. Of these, six remained in 1940 and these were destroyed by the Germans.
Type: Heavy tank.
Engine: 2 Maybach, 6-in-line (each), 250 bhp. Liquid.
Transmission: Petrol-electric system with 4 electric motors, steered by varying the speed of track motors and additional track brakes. 12 kph.
Arms: 75 mm gun, 4 machine guns. 13 crew.
Dimensions: 10.27 m×2.95 m×4.04 m. 68,000 kg approx.

1920s (GB)
15 pdr mortar

A close-support weapon intended to accompany tanks and capable of firing smoke. It was based on the contemporary standard Vickers medium tank Mk II.
Type: Self-propelled artillery.
Engine: Armstrong-Siddeley V8, 8-in-V, 90 bhp at 1,750 rpm. Air.
Transmission: 4-speed gearbox and 2-speed planetary transmission, clutch and brake steering. 18 mph, 10 mph cross country.
Arms: 15 pdr mortar. 5 crew.
Dimensions: 17 ft 6 in×9 ft 1½ in×8 ft 10 in. 13 tons approx.

1920s Citroen/Schneider (F)

Schneider P16

This half-track vehicle was also known as Citroen-Kegresse M28. It consisted of a Citroen-built chassis with Panhard engine and Kegresse-Hinstin tracked rear bogie, fitted with a Schneider armoured hull with rotating turret.

Type: Armoured car.
Engine: Panhard 15CV SS, 4-in-line, 50 bhp. Liquid.
Transmission: 6 F 6 R, steering by front wheels (duplicate controls at rear). 55 kph.
Arms: 37 mm gun, 1 machine gun. 3 crew.
Dimensions: 4.3 m × 1.6 m × 2.45 m. 5,800 kg approx.

1930s Somua (F)
MCG11

One of many types of half-track vehicles produced by the French industry during the interwar period. The MCG11 was a modification of Somua's MCG5, adapted as a prime mover for the 155 mm gun (155 *court*). It featured a 1½ ton winch.
Type: Artillery tractor.

Engine: Somua 4.7 litre, 4-in-line, 60 bhp. Liquid.
Transmission: 5 F 1 R, steering by front wheels. 31 kph.
Crew: 2.
Dimensions: 4.55 m × 1.9 m. 3,500 kg (basic chassis).

1930s Renault (F)
1931R

Known officially as *Chenillette de Ravitaillement d'Infanterie, Modèle 1931R*, this armoured supply tractor was in production until 1940 by which time AMX (l'Atelier de Construction d'Issy-les-Moulineaux, formed in 1936 by nationalizing the Renault plant at 247, Quai d'Issy-les-Moulineaux) had delivered 6,000 units. They were normally used with a tracked trailer, as shown.

Type: Tractor.
Engine: Renault 85, 4-in-line, 35 bhp at 2,400 rpm. Liquid.
Transmission: 3 F 1 R, track brake steering. 20 kph.
Crew: 2.
Dimensions: 2.7 m × 1.7 m × 1.03 m. 2,100 kg approx.

1930s Daimler-Benz (D)

12 ton Sd. Kfz. 8

The original version of the heavy semi-track artillery prime mover, produced in 1934 by Daimler-Benz with model designation DB s 7. Subsequent modernized versions included the DB s 8 (1936–7), DB9 (1938–9) and DB10 (1939–44). There were also lighter (1, 3, 5 and 8 ton) and heavier (18 ton) editions, all following the same basic design configuration. The vehicle shown tows a 15 cm gun.
Type: Artillery tractor.
Engine: Maybach DSO 8, 12-in-V, 150 bhp at 2,300 rpm. Liquid.
Transmission: 8 F 2 R 4-speed gearbox and 2-speed auxiliary gearbox, steering by front wheels and mechanical final drive brakes. 50 kph.
Crew: 12.
Dimensions: 6.8 m × 2.35 m × 2.2 m. 12,600 kg approx.

1930s ČKD (ČS)

ČKD VZOR 33/Praga P1

Claimed to be the first full-track AFV produced in Czechoslovakia, this vehicle was evolved from the British Carden-Loyd Mk VI two-man tankette, of which about 100 had been supplied commercially to many other countries. Armour thickness was 5 to 12 mm.
Type: Light tank (tankette).
Engine: Praga AN, 4-in-line, 31 bhp at 2,800 rpm. Liquid.
Transmission: 4 F 1 R, track brake steering. 45 kph, 20 kph cross country.
Arms: 2 machine guns. 2 crew.
Dimensions: 2.6 m × 1.7 m × 1.7 m. 2,500 kg approx.

1930s Vickers-Armstrong (GB)
Mk VIA

This was one of the final developments of the Vickers-Armstrong/Carden-Loyd series of light tanks, originated in the late 1920s. The Mk VI series tanks (Mk VI to VIC) were produced during 1936–40 and used by all divisional Cavalry recce regiments at the beginning of World War II.
Type: Light tank.
Engine: Meadows, 6-in-line, 88 bhp at 2,800 rpm. Liquid.
Transmission: 5 F 1 R, clutch and brake steering. 35 mph, 25 mph cross country.
Arms: 2 machine guns. 3 crew.
Dimensions: 12 ft 11½ in × 6 ft 9 in × 7 ft 3½ in. 11,740 lbs approx.

1930s (D)
Sd. Kfz. 101, Ausführung A

The *Pz. Kw. I* was the main equipment of the German tank regiments during 1935–40. It was a lightly armoured vehicle (13 mm armour thickness). Later production vehicles (*Ausf. B*) had a more powerful Maybach engine of 100 bhp.
Type: Light tank.
Engine: Krupp M304, flat-4, 57 bhp at 2,500 rpm. Air.
Transmission: 5 F 1 R, clutch brake steering. 37 kph.
Arms: 2 machine guns. 2 crew.
Dimensions: 4.02 m × 2.06 m × 1.72 m. 5,400 kg approx.

See previous page

1930s (USSR)
T28C

The T28 saw service in the Russo–Finnish war and on the Eastern Front until 1941. There were three turrets, namely the main turret and two auxiliary machine gun turrets at the front.
Type: Medium tank.
Engine: Liberty M17L, 12-in-V, 500 bhp at 1,460 rpm. Liquid.
Transmission: 5 F 1 R, clutch and brake steering. 24 kph.
Arms: 76.2 mm gun, 3 machine guns. 6 crew.
Dimensions: 7.35 m × 2.76 m × 2.8 m. 32,000 kg approx.

WW II Steyr (A/D)
RSO/01

Designed by Steyr for use by the German Army on the eastern front, the majority had a conventional truck-type steel cab. The vehicle shown has a simplified cab. Klöckner-Deutz-Magirus in Germany built the same vehicle, but with a 4 cyl. Deutz diesel engine and soft-top cab (RSO/03). A half-track version of the latter appeared shortly after the war, called *'Wald-schlepper'*.
Type: Tractor.
Engine: Steyr 1500A, 8-in-V, 70 bhp at 2,500 rpm. Air.
Transmission: 4 F 1 R (overdrive top), hydraulic steering brakes. 17 kph.
Crew: 2.
Dimensions: 4.42 m × 2 m × 2.53 m. 3,500 kg approx.

WW II ČKD Praga (ČS)
T6-SS

Seventy-three were produced in 1944 for *Deutsche Wehrmacht*. It had a 7.75 litre petrol engine, a 6 ton winch with 60 m of cable and drawbar pull of 5,500 kg. Payload was 1,000 kg. During the late 1930s, Praga supplied artillery tractors of various sizes to many governments.
Type: Artillery tractor.
Engine: Praga AE, 6-in-line, 110 bhp at 1,800 rpm. Liquid.
Transmission: 4 F 1 R with 2-speed transfer case, track brake steering.
31 kph.
Crew: 2+8.
Dimensions: 5.1 m×2 m×2.5 m.
7,500 kg approx.

WW II ČKD (ČS)
ČKD Raupenschlepper

This tractor appeared in 1944 (prototype in 1943) and was based on the ČKD/Praga TNH light tank. It had an armour-plate hull with open rear compartment (provided with bows for canvas tilt). It is believed that only a few were built, for the German Army.
Type: Artillery tractor.

Engine: Tatra T103 (diesel), 12-in-V, 230 bhp at 2,250 rpm. Air.
Transmission: 4 F 1 R, controlled differential steering. 35 kph.
Crew: 2.
Dimensions: 5.05 m × 2.3 m × 2.2 m approx. 12,000 kg approx.

WW II Fordson Roadless (GB)

Half-track

The basis of this machine, used by the RAF, was a Fordson agricultural tractor. It was converted to the half-track configuration by Roadless Traction Ltd. The tracks were rubber-jointed and the track plates were 13 in wide. Ground contact area was 1,040 sq in. It was fitted with a Hesford Major or Minor winch at front or rear respectively.

Type: Tractor.

Engine: Ford 4.38 litre, 4-in-line, 45 bhp. Liquid.

Transmission: 3 F 1 R, front wheel steering. 6.3 mph.

Crew: 1.

Dimensions: 10 ft 8 in×5 ft 9 in×4 ft 7 in. 3¼ tons approx.

WW II Vauxhall (GB)

¾-track 'Traclat'

Patterned on German Sd. Kfz. 7 medium-type semi-track tractor, the initial work was by Morris-Commercial Cars Ltd. Prototypes (6) were produced by Vauxhall Motors Ltd, designated Bedford BT (Bedford Tractor). It was intended for towing 25 pdr, 17 pdr and Bofors AA guns.

Type: Artillery tractor.

Engine: Twin Bedford 3.5 litre, 6-in-line (each), 68 bhp at 3,000 rpm. Liquid.

Transmission: 5 F 1 R, controlled differential and front wheel steering. 30 mph.

Crew: 2+5.

Dimensions: 21 ft×7 ft 6 in×8 ft 11 in. 6¾ tons approx.

WW II (GB)
'Loyd'

The 'Loyd' carrier was a rear-engined multi-purpose vehicle with several components in common with the Bren and Universal Carrier. However, it featured extra bogie wheels, front drive (but brakes on all four sprockets), tiller steering and a 'soft-skin' body. A rescued specimen shown is on its way to the Myreton Motor Museum near Aberlady, East Lothian in 1972.
Type: Artillery tractor.
Engine: Ford V8, 8-in-V, 85 bhp at 3,800 rpm. Liquid.
Transmission: 4 F 1 R driving front sprockets, Ford steering by drum brakes on front and rear sprockets. 30 mph.
Crew: 1.
Dimensions: 13 ft 7 in×6 ft 9½ in×7 ft (reducible to 4 ft 8 in). 3½–4 tons.

WW II (GB)
'Crusader' II, Mk I

A conversion of the 'Crusader' II tank for use as high-speed tractor for 17 pdr anti-tank gun. The vehicle was equipped with gun crew seats and ammunition lockers.
Type: Artillery tractor.
Engine: Nuffield Liberty, 12-in-V, 340 bhp at 1,500 rpm. Liquid.
Transmission: 4 F 1 R, Wilson epicyclic steering gear with skid brakes, pneumatically controlled. 27 mph.
Crew: 2+gun crew.
Dimensions: 20 ft 8 in×8 ft 10 in×7 ft 6 in (with canopy raised). 18½ tons approx.

WW II (J)

6 ton, Type 98 (1938)

Used by the Japanese Army for towing 105 mm gun and howitzer and 150 mm howitzer. Shown after capture by Australian 29th Brigade, 3rd Inf. Div., hauling a train of 'Jeep'-trailers along a 'road' in Bougainville, 1944.
Type: Artillery tractor.
Engine: Isuzu (diesel), 6-in-line, 110 bhp at 1,700 rpm. Liquid.
Transmission: 4 F 1 R, clutch brake steering. 24 kph.
Crew: 7.
Dimensions: 4.3 m × 2.05 m × 1.9 m. 6,900 kg approx.

WW II Allis-Chalmers (USA)

Half-track, M7

Originally known as T26E4, it was produced by Allis-Chalmers Mfg. Co. of Milwaukee, Wisc., utilizing Willys 'Jeep' engine, gearbox, etc. It was used by US Army Air Force ground search and rescue units in snow areas of America's far North. The front wheels could be replaced by skis (shown in their alternative position as mud/snow guards).
Type: Snow tractor.
Engine: Willys MB442, 4-in-line, 63 bhp at 3,900 rpm. Liquid.
Transmission: 3 F 1 R, front wheel/ski steering. 40 mph.
Crew: 2.
Dimensions: 136 in × 63 in × 64 in (reducible to 43 in). 2,500 lbs approx.

WW II Caterpillar (USA)
Tractor, Heavy, M1

Produced by Caterpillar Tractor Co (tractors in same category also produced by Allis-Chalmers [HD 10W] and International Harvester [TD18]). Shown pulling amphibious trailer along a beach 'somewhere in the Pacific area', September 1944 (USMC).
Type: Tractor.

Engine: Caterpillar D7 (D–8800 diesel), 4-in-line, 80 drawbar hp at 1,000 rpm. Liquid.
Transmission: 5 F 4 R, controlled differential steering.
Crew: 2.
Dimensions: 180 in approx. × 100 in × 80 in (top of air intake). 25,470 lbs (gross).

WW II International (USA)
13 ton M5

Produced by International Harvester Co. and used for towing artillery (105 mm, 155 mm, 4.5 in) over roads and rough terrain. Shown as used by Japanese Self Defence Forces in the 1960s.
Type: Artillery tractor.
Engine: Continental R6572, 6-in-line, 207 bhp at 2,900 rpm. Liquid.
Transmission: 4 F 1 R with 2-speed auxiliary gearbox, controlled differential steering. 35 mph.
Arms: 1 machine gun. 9 crew.
Dimensions: 191 in × 100 in × 104 in. 28,300 lbs (gross).

WW II International (USA)
13 ton M5A1

A variant of soft-top M5, with steel canopy top, used for towing 105 mm and 155 mm artillery. The M5A2 and M5A3 were similar to M5 and M5A1 respectively but with 21 in tracks and horizontal volute spring suspension. These developments were used throughout the 1950s by several nations.
Type: Artillery tractor.
Engine: Continental R6572, 6-in-line, 207 bhp at 2,900 rpm. Liquid.
Transmission: 4 F 1 R with 2-speed auxiliary gearbox, controlled differential steering. 30 mph.
Arms: 1 machine gun. 11 crew.
Dimensions: 195½ in × 100 in × 104 in. 30,405 lbs approx.

WW II Allis-Chalmers (USA)
18 ton M4

Produced by Allis-Chalmers Mfg. Co. and used for towing artillery pieces (3 in AA gun, 90 mm AA gun, 155 mm gun, 8 in howitzer and 240 mm howitzer). The picture shows tractor towing 90 mm gun over Bailey bridge crossing River Seine, France, in 1944.
Type: Artillery tractor.

Engine: Waukesha 145GZ, 6-in-line, 190 bhp at 2,100 rpm. Liquid.
Transmission: 3 F 1 R × 3 with torque converter, controlled differential steering. 35 mph.
Arms: 1 machine gun. 11 crew.
Dimensions: 210 in × 97 in × 107 in. 31,400 lbs approx.

WW II Allis-Chalmers (USA)
38 ton M6

Produced by Allis-Chalmers Mfg. Co. and designed as prime mover for 4.7 in AA gun, 8 in gun and 240 mm howitzer. The low centre of gravity enabled it to climb slopes as steep as 30°, depending on the kind of footing available and the load being pulled.
Type: Artillery tractor.

Engine: 2 Waukesha 145GZ, 6-in-line (each), 190 bhp at 2,100 rpm. Liquid.
Transmission: Twin-Disc torque converters, 2 F 1 R, controlled differential steering. 21 mph.
Arms: 1 machine gun. 10 crew.
Dimensions: 258 in × 120½ in × 104 in. 76,000 lbs gross.

WW II (USSR)
S-65 'Stalinets-65'

Basically an agricultural type track-laying machine, the 'Stalinets-65' was widely used for artillery towing. The two-door cab shown was usually fitted. The slightly larger 'Stalinets-80' looked similar.
Type: Artillery tractor.
Engine: Stalinets diesel, 6-in-line, 65 bhp. Liquid.
Transmission: 5 F 1 R, controlled differential steering. 10 kph.
Crew: 2.
Dimensions: 4.09 m × 2.42 m × 2.8 m. 11,200 kg.

WW II (USSR)
STZ 'Komsomolets'

This tractor had an armoured cab at the front and the engine centrally mounted at the rear. Over the engine were two rows of three folding crew seats, back to back.
Type: Artillery tractor.
Engine: GAZ–M1, 4-in-line, 50 bhp at 2,800 rpm. Liquid.
Transmission: 4 F 1 R, clutch and brake steering. 30 kph.
Arms: 1 machine gun. 2+6 crew.
Dimensions: 3.45 m × 1.86 m × 1.4 m. 4,200 kg.

WW II Rheinmetall (D)
Land-Wasser-Schlepper

Only 21 of these lightly armoured L-W-S amphibious tractors were produced for the *Wehrmacht* shortly before the war at the Boizenburg/Elbe shipyard of Rheinmetall. The vehicle shown took part in the invasion of the Netherlands. (Photo taken in Terneuzen, summer 1940)
Type: Amphibian.
Engine: Maybach HL108TR, 12-in-V, 280–300 bhp. Liquid.
Transmission: 5 F 1 R, controlled differential steering. Water propulsion by 2 large propellers mounted in front of 2 rudder blades at the rear. 35 kph, 12.5 kph in water.
Crew: 3.
Dimensions: 8.6 m × 3.16 m × 3.15 m. 13,000 kg approx.

WW II Nuffield (GB)
'Argosy'

Three prototypes were developed by Nuffield to meet certain WD specifications, including the requirement to have a hold with a 9 ton payload capability in any sea and at the same time be able to house the 17 pdr gun. Subsequent requirement for rear-end ramp loading, virtually impossible within the 'Argosy' envelopment, brought the project to an end.
Type: Amphibian.
Engine: Nuffield Liberty, 12-in-V, 340 bhp at 1,500 rpm. Liquid.
Transmission: 4 F 1 R, controlled differential steering. Twin 2 ft diameter propellers for sea-going. 20 mph, 4 knots in water.

WW II Nuffield (GB)
'Neptune'

The British Army was supplied with quantities of the US LVT (Landing Vehicle, Tracked) under Lend-Lease. In order not to be entirely dependent on American supplies in case of emergencies, Morris-Commercial Cars Ltd in conjunction with Nuffield Mechanizations, produced the 'Neptune' which was fundamentally similar to the LVT; 2,000 were ordered but few had been delivered when the war ended.

Type: Amphibian.
Engine: Meadows NEP/I or II, flat-12, 280 bhp. Liquid.
Transmission: Meadows 55 4 F 1 R, controlled differential steering. 19 mph, 5½ mph in water.
Crew: 2.
Dimensions: 30 ft 2½ in × 11 ft 8 in × 10 ft 6½ in. 17 tons approx.

WW II Studebaker (USA)
M29C

Popularly known as the 'Water Weasel', this was the amphibious edition of the Studebaker 'Weasel'. The picture shows vehicle with hardtop superstructure (post-war modification) of the US Marine Corps. during an exercise in 1947.
Type: Amphibian.
Engine: Studebaker Champion 6–170, 6-in-line, 65 bhp at 3,600 rpm. Liquid.
Transmission: 3 F 1 R with 2-speed final drive at rear, skid steering with mechanical brakes in differential. 36 mph, 4 mph in water.
Crew: 2+2.
Dimensions: 192 in × 67 in × 71 in (reducible to 54 in). 4,778 lbs approx.

WW II (USA)

LVT3 'Bushmaster'

Known as the 'Bushmaster', this vehicle was developed by Borg Warner. It had a stern ramp and two Cadillac engines, one in each side pontoon. The LVT4 was similar in many respects but had a Continental radial aircraft-type engine immediately behind the driving compartment. A preserved LVT3 is shown from England.

Type: Amphibian.
Engine: 2 Cadillac Series 42, 8-in-V (each), 110 bhp. Liquid.
Transmission: Hydra-Matic 4F1R automatic transmissions, controlled differential steering. 17 mph, 6 mph in water.
Arms: 2–3 machine guns. 3 crew.
Dimensions: 294 in × 134 in × 119 in. 26,600 lbs approx.

WW II (USA)
LVT(A)4

A modification of the LVT(A)1 which, in turn, was a modification of the LVT2 open-top landing vehicle. The turret and howitzer were the same as on the M8 Gun Motor Carriage. It was used in the Pacific war during 1944–5. Armour thickness was $\frac{1}{4}$ to $\frac{1}{2}$ in.
Type: Amphibian.

Engine: Continental W670–9A, 7 cyl. single-row radial, 250 bhp at 2,400 rpm. Air.
Transmission: 5 F 1 R, controlled differential steering. 16 mph, 7 mph in water.
Arms: 75 mm howitzer, 1 machine gun. 6 crew.
Dimensions: 314 in × 130 in × 123 in. 40,000 lbs approx.

WW II Demag (D)
Sd. Kfz. 250

The l.SPW was produced by Demag (Model D7p) and was a modification of their unarmoured 1 ton Sd.Kfz.10 semi-track tractor (Model D7). It was the basis for a range of light armoured vehicles, totalling some 12 variants. There was a similar 'family' based on the somewhat larger Sd.Kfz.251 vehicle.
Type: Armoured personnel carrier.
Engine: Maybach HL42 TRKM, 6-in-line, 100 bhp at 2,800 rpm. Liquid.
Transmission: Maybach semi-automatic Variorex 7 F 3 R, steered by front wheels and controlled differential. 65 kph.
Arms: 1 machine gun. 6 crew.
Dimensions: 4.56 m × 1.95 m × 1.66 m. 5,000 kg approx.

WW II (GB)

Universal Carrier No. 1, Mk I

The Universal Carrier was used for a variety of purposes and formed the basis for other applications, e.g. armoured observation post, mortar carrier, flame thrower, etc. Carrier, Universal, No. 2 had an 85 bhp engine and No. 3 had a 95 bhp engine (all Ford V8s). (IWM photo H12186)

Type: Tracked carrier.
Engine: Ford V8, 8-in-V, 65 bhp. Liquid.
Transmission: 4 F 1 R, steering-wheel operated moving cross tube, warping the tracks and brakes with differential for tight turns. 30 mph.
Arms: 1 machine gun (not usually used from vehicle). 3 crew.
Dimensions: 12 ft×6 ft 9 in×5 ft 3 in. $3\frac{3}{4}$–$4\frac{1}{4}$ tons.

WW II (GB)

Carrier, AOP No. 1, Mks I & II

A variant of the popular infantry carrier, fitted out for use as an armoured observation post (AOP). A cable drum was fitted to the rear of the vehicle. The Mk III version was a variant of the later Universal Carrier.

Type: Tracked carrier.

Engine: Ford V8, 8-in-V, 65 bhp. Liquid.

Transmission: 4 F 1 R, steering-wheel operated moving cross tube, warping the tracks and brakes with differential for tight turns. 30 mph.

Crew: 3.

Dimensions: 12 ft × 6 ft 9 in × 5 ft 3 in. $3\frac{3}{4}$–$4\frac{1}{4}$ tons.

WW II Studebaker (USA)
M29

Produced by the Studebaker Corporation for use as transporter of personnel and cargo over snow, and for limited operation on the ground, it was popularly known as the 'Weasel'. The engine was located alongside the driver, on the right. Vehicle shown had 15 in tracks, later models had 20 in tracks.
Type: Tracked carrier.
Engine: Studebaker Champion 6–170, 6-in-line, 65 bhp at 3,600 rpm. Liquid.
Transmission: 3 F 1 R with 2-speed final drive at rear, skid steering with mechanical brakes in differential.
36 mph.
Crew: 2.
Dimensions: 126 in × 66 in (71 in with 20 in tracks) × 71 in (reducible to 54 in).
4,540 lbs approx.

WW II Ford (USA)
Universal T16

This looked similar to British Universal Carrier but it had lever steering, extra bogie wheels and many differences of detail. It was produced by the Ford Motor Co. in the USA, for the British Army. The specimen shown was one of 320 in service with the Swiss Army after the war. Some of these had a Swiss-built superstructure with tilt.

Type: Tracked carrier.
Engine: Ford GAU370, 8-in-V, 100 bhp at 3,800 rpm. Liquid.
Transmission: 4 F 1 R, skid steering by levers. 33 mph.
Crew: 4–9.
Dimensions: 155 in × 83 in × 62 in. 7,756 lbs (gross 9,500 lbs).

WW II (GB)
Mk VII 'Tetrach' I

Designed by Vickers in 1937–8 (then known as 'Purdah'). Quantity production during 1940–1 by Metropolitan-Cammell. Its armour was 14–16 mm thick.
Type: Light tank.
Engine: Meadows MAT, 12 cyl., 165 bhp at 2,700 rpm. Liquid.
Transmission: 8-wheel steering with flexing tracks and differential brakes for tight turns. 40 mph, 28 mph cross country.
Arms: 2 pdr gun, 1 machine gun, 2 4 in smoke dischargers. 3 crew.
Dimensions: 14 ft 1½ in × 7 ft 7 in × 6 ft 11½ in. 7½ tons approx.

WW II (GB)

Mk VIII 'Harry Hopkins' I

A Vickers design of 1941. The armour was a maximum of 38 mm thick. Quantity production by Metropolitan-Cammell in 1944, it was used as a basis for the 'Alecto' SP 95 mm howitzer.
Type: Light tank.
Engine: Meadows MAT, 12 cyl., 150 bhp. Liquid.
Transmission: 8-wheel steering with flexing tracks and differential brakes for tight turns. 30 mph, 20 mph cross country.
Arms: 2 pdr gun, 1 machine gun. 3 crew.
Dimensions: 14 ft×8 ft 10½ in×6 ft 11 in. 8–9 tons.

WW II Fiat-Ansaldo (I)

L6/40

The L6/40 was designed and developed in the late 1930s and saw action with the Italian Army in North Africa and Russia from 1941. There was also an SP derivative, the Semovente 47/32. They were produced by Fiat-Ansaldo.

Type: Light tank.

Engine: Spa 18VT, 4-in-line, 68 bhp at 2,500 rpm. Liquid.

Transmission: 4 F 1 R with reduction gear, clutch brake steering. 40 kph.

Arms: 20 mm gun, 1 machine gun. 2 crew.

Dimensions: 3.78 m × 1.95 m × 2 m. 7,000 kg approx.

WW II (USA)
M5A1

The M5A1 was standardized in 1942 and was a development from the M3 light tank. It was developed by the Cadillac Division of General Motors and built by them as well as by Massey-Harris and American Car & Foundry. Armour was 0.5–2 in thick.
Type: Light tank.
Engine: 2 Cadillac Series 42, 8-in-V (each), 110 bhp. Liquid.
Transmission: Hydramatic automatic transmission (each), controlled differential steering. 40 mph, 25 mph cross country.
Arms: 37 mm gun, 2 machine guns. 4 crew.
Dimensions: 190 in × 90 in × 90 in. 33,900 lbs approx.

WW II Marmon-Herrington (USA)
Airborne, M22 'Locust'

Produced by Marmon-Herrington in 1943–4, Great Britain received a large number and named it the 'Locust'. Some were used in the Rhine crossing operations in March 1945 (British 6th Airborne Division).
Type: Light tank.
Engine: Lycoming 0–435–T, flat-6, 162 bhp. Air.
Transmission: 4 F 1 R, controlled differential steering. 42 mph, 30 mph cross country.
Arms: 37 mm gun, 1 machine gun, 1 sub-machine gun. 3 crew.
Dimensions: 155 in × 88 in × 68½ in. 16,400 lbs (net airborne, 15,800 lbs).

WW II (USA)
M24 'Chaffee'

Produced by Cadillac and Massey-Harris from March 1944 and used by several nations until the 1970s. The specimen shown is French DTAT modification of the late 1960s with 90 mm gun for fin-stabilized anti-tank shells.
Type: Light tank.
Engine: 2 Cadillac 44T24, 8-in-V (each), 110 bhp. Liquid.
Transmission: 2 Hydramatic 4 F 1 R automatic transmissions with 2-speed transfer case, controlled differential steering.
Arms (original): 75 mm gun, 3 machine guns, 1 smoke mortar. 4–5 crew.
Dimensions: 198 in × 116 in × 109 in. 40,500 lbs approx.

WW II (USSR)
Amphibious T40

This was a light amphibious tank of all-welded construction, first produced in 1940. The engine was on the right-hand side and the armoured air intake cover is clearly visible. The turret was off-set to the left. The vehicle featured built-in buoyancy tanks.
Type: Light tank.
Engine: GAZ–202, 6-in-line, 85 bhp at 3,600 rpm. Liquid.
Transmission: 4 F 1 R, clutch and brake steering. 45 kph.
Arms: 20 mm gun, 1 machine gun. 2 crew.
Dimensions: 4.1 m × 2.3 m × 1.7 m. 5½ tons approx.

WW II (D)

Panzer IV

One of 10 variants of the widely used *'Panzer IV'* range of medium tanks, produced from 1936 until the end of the war by Krupp and Vomag. The latest versions were also made by Steyr in Austria and Praga in Czechoslovakia.
Type: Medium tank.
Engine: Maybach HL 120TRM, 12-in-V, 300 bhp at 3,000 rpm. Liquid.
Transmission: ZF-Aphon 6 F 1 R, controlled differential steering. 38 kph.
Arms: 7.5 cm gun, 2 machine guns. 5 crew.
Dimensions: 7.02 m × 2.88 m × 2.68 m. 25,000 kg (gross).

WW II (USA)
M2A1

Fewer than 100 of these were produced by Rock Island Arsenal during 1940–1 but it was obsolete by the time it appeared. It was the immediate predecessor of the mass-produced M3 and M4 ('Sherman') medium tanks.
Type: Medium tank.
Engine: Wright Whirlwind, 9-radial, 400 bhp. Air.
Transmission: 5 F 1 R, controlled differential steering.
26 mph, 17 mph cross country.
Arms: 37 mm gun, 8 machine guns. 6 crew.
Dimensions: 210 in × 102 in × 111 in. 47,040 lbs approx.

WW II (USA)

M3 'General Lee'

Some tanks were powered by a 350 bhp Guiberson T1400 diesel engine. Nearly 5,000 were built during 1941–2, the majority by Detroit Arsenal. The M3A1 was similar except for a cast instead of a riveted hull. Several other variants existed, including the 'Grant', which was the M3 with a different turret for the British Army.
Type: Medium tank.
Engine: Continental R975–EC2, 9-radial, 400 bhp. Air.
Transmission: 5 F 1 R, controlled differential steering. 25 mph, 16 mph cross country.
Arms: 75 mm gun (right front), 37 mm gun (turret), 3 machine guns, 1 submachine gun. 7 crew.
Dimensions: 222 in × 107 in × 123 in. 60,000 lbs approx.

WW II (USA)
M4A3 'Sherman'

One of the many variants of the famous range of M4 'Sherman' tanks. This particular model was built by Ford. From 1942–6, over 40,000 AFVs (tanks, SPs, etc.) were built on this chassis by several manufacturers, using different types of engines, armament, etc.
Type: Medium tank.

Engine: Ford GAA, 8-in-V, 450–500 bhp at 2,600 rpm. Liquid.
Transmission: 5 F 1 R, controlled differential steering. 26 mph, 15 mph cross country.
Arms: 75 mm gun, 3 machine guns. 5 crew.
Dimensions: 247 in × 105 in × 125 in. 69,500 lbs approx.

WW II (USA)
M26 'Pershing'

Originally known as Heavy Tank M26, this was the first US tank to have the M3 90 mm tank gun. They were being issued to US armoured divisions during the last six weeks of the war.
Type: Medium tank.
Engine: Ford GAF, 8-in-V, 500 bhp at 2,600 rpm. Liquid.
Transmission: Torqmatic 3 F 1 R, controlled differential steering. 30 mph, 18 mph cross country.
Arms: 90 mm gun, 3 machine guns. 5 crew.
Dimensions: 268 in (gun in travelling position) × 137 in × 109 in. 92,000 lbs approx.

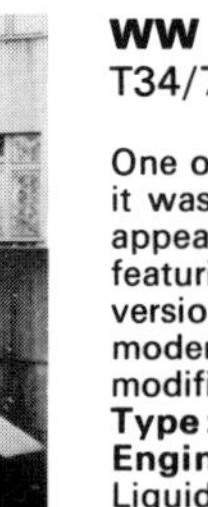

WW II (USSR)
T34/76E

One of the most successful tanks of World War II, during which it was produced in large numbers. The 76E model shown first appeared in 1943 and was one of the final production models, featuring many improvements over the earlier T34/76A–D versions. Later they were superseded by the 'upgunned' and modernized T34/85, which had an 85 mm gun and other modifications.
Type: Medium tank.
Engine: V–2–34 (diesel), 12-in-V, 500 bhp at 1,800 rpm. Liquid.
Transmission: 4 F 1 R, clutch and brake steering. 50 kph, 40 kph cross country.
Arms: 76.2 mm gun, 2 machine guns. 4 crew.
Dimensions: 5.92 m × 3 m × 2.4 m. 31,500 kg approx.

WW II (GB)

Cruiser Mks IV & IVA (A13 Mk II)

The main producer of the Cruiser Mk IV was Nuffield Mechanizations. It superseded the 1938 Mk III type, of which it was an improved development, in 1939. A tank is shown being loaded on to a Scammell 30 ton transporter.
Type: Cruiser tank.
Engine: Nuffield Liberty, 12-in-V, 340 bhp at 1,500 rpm. Liquid.
Transmission: 4 F 1 R, clutch and brake steering. 30 mph, 14 mph cross country.
Arms: 2 pdr gun, 1 machine gun. 4 crew.
Dimensions: 19 ft 9 in × 8 ft 4 in × 8 ft 6 in. 14½ tons approx.

WW II (GB)

Mk V 'Covenanter' III (A13 Mk III)

The 'Covenanter' was produced in relatively small quantities (under 1,800) and was not used operationally. There were several Marks and some variants including a bridgelayer. Maximum armour thickness was 50 mm.
Type: Cruiser tank.

Engine: Meadows DAV, flat-12, 300 bhp. Liquid.
Transmission: 4 F 1 R, 2 Wilson 2-speed epicyclic steering units, one each side of gearbox. 31 mph.
Arms: 2 pdr gun, 1 machine gun, 2 in bomb thrower. 4 crew.
Dimensions: 19 ft 6 in × 8 ft 7 in × 7 ft 4 in. 18 tons approx.

WW II (GB)

Mk VI 'Crusader' III (A15)

Designed by Nuffield Mechanizations and built by them and 9 other manufacturers. Well over 5,000 were produced during 1940–3. There were many modifications and variations such as the SP AA guns.
Type: Cruiser tank.
Engine: Nuffield Liberty, 12-in-V, 340 bhp at 1,500 rpm. Liquid.
Transmission: 4 F 1 R, 2 Wilson epicyclic steering units with skid brakes, pneumatically controlled. 27 mph, 15 mph cross country.
Arms: 6 pdr gun, 1 machine gun, 2 in smoke mortar. 3 crew.
Dimensions: 20 ft 7½ in × 8 ft 8 in × 7 ft 4 in. 19 tons approx.

WW II (GB)

Mk VIII 'Centaur' I (A27L)

The 'Centaur' was externally similar to the 'Cavalier' and 'Cromwell' tanks. A number were converted to 'Cromwells' by retro-fitting the Rolls-Royce Meteor engine. These tanks were known as 'Cromwell' III (originally 'Cromwell' X).
Type: Cruiser tank.

Engine: Liberty Mk V, 12-in-V, 395 bhp. Liquid.
Transmission: 5 F 1 R, Merritt Brown controlled differential steering. 28 mph, 16 mph cross country.
Arms: 6 pdr, 1–2 machine guns. 5 crew.
Dimensions: 21 ft 10 in×9 ft 6 in×7 ft 9 in. 28 tons approx.

WW II (GB)

Mk VIII 'Cromwell' III (A27M)

The 'Cromwell' was similar to the 'Centaur' tank, the main exception being the fitting of a modified Rolls-Royce Meteor aircraft engine. Numerically it was one of the most important British cruiser tanks of its time.

Type: Cruiser tank.

Engine: Rolls-Royce Meteor, 12-in-V, 600 bhp. Liquid.

Transmission: Merritt Brown 5 F 1 R, Lockheed controlled steering. 40 mph, 18 mph cross country.

Arms: 6 pdr gun, 2 machine guns. 5 crew.

Dimensions: 21 ft 9 in × 9 ft 6 in × 7 ft 9 in. 27½ tons approx.

WW II (GB)
'Challenger' I (A30)

The 'Challenger' was specially built for the heavy 17 pdr anti-tank gun. Many of the mechanical components were the same as the 'Cromwell' but the hull was longer and wider and the turret was, of course, of a special design. There was an extra bogie wheel on each side.

Type: Cruiser tank.

Engine: Rolls-Royce Meteor, 12-in-V, 600 bhp. Liquid.

Transmission: 5 F 1 R, epicyclic gear steering operated by hydraulic brakes. 32 mph, 15 mph cross country.

Arms: 17 pdr gun, 1 machine gun co-axially mounted. 5 crew.

Dimensions: 26 ft 4 in × 9 ft 6½ in × 8 ft 9 in. 31½ tons approx.

WW II (GB)
'Comet' I (A34)

The 'Comet' first appeared late in 1944 and saw active service with the 11th Armoured Division after the Rhine crossing of March 1945. It was a virtual redesign of the earlier Type A27 cruiser tanks 'Centaur' and 'Cromwell' and was a product of Leyland. Production models had track return rollers, unlike the prototype vehicle shown.
Type: Cruiser tank.
Engine: Rolls-Royce Meteor, 12-in-V, 600 bhp. Liquid.
Transmission: Controlled differential steering. 29 mph, 16 mph cross country.
Arms: 77 mm gun (compact 17 pdr), 2 machine guns. 5 crew.
Dimensions: 25 ft 1½ in × 10 ft × 8 ft 9½ in. 35 tons approx.

WW II (GB)

Mk II 'Matilda' II (A12)

Designed by Vulcan Foundry and produced by them and other manufacturers. The 'Matilda' I was similar except for having a Vickers 0.303 in machine gun (instead of Besa 7.92 mm). 'Matildas' III, IV and V were generally similar to the Mark II but had twin Leyland 95 bhp diesel engines.

Type: Infantry tank.

Engine: 2 AEC A183/A184 (diesel), 6-in-line (each), 87 bhp at 2,000 rpm. Liquid.

Transmission: Wilson 6 F 1 R epicyclic gearbox, Rackham steering clutches.

Arms: 2 pdr gun and 1 machine gun. 4 crew.

Dimensions: 19 ft 9 in × 8 ft 6 in × 8 ft. 26½ tons approx.

WW II (GB)

Mk III 'Valentine' IX

Designed by Vickers and built by Vickers and two other manufacturers, it was one of the most important British tanks of World War II. It was also produced in Canada, mainly for Russia (Lend-Lease). Early productions had an AEC engine and 2 pdr gun.

Type: Infantry tank.

Engine: General Motors 6–71 (2-stroke diesel), 6-in-line, 138 bhp. Liquid.

Transmission: Skid steering by clutch and brake. 15 mph, 8 mph cross country.

Arms: 6 pdr gun, 2 4 in smoke dischargers, Bren and Thompson machine guns. 3 crew.

Dimensions: 19 ft 4 in × 8 ft 9½ in × 7 ft 1 in. 17 tons approx.

WW II (GB)

Mk IV 'Churchill' I (A22)

The first production model (1941) of the famous 'Churchill' tank, designed by Vauxhall Motors. It was followed by many improved versions and there were several variants for specialist roles. 'Churchill' II was similar to the vehicle shown but was without the howitzer (in the nose) and with an extra Besa machine gun.

Type: Infantry tank.
Engine: Bedford Twin-Six, flat-12, 350 bhp at 2,200 rpm. Liquid.
Transmission: 4 F 1 R, epicyclic reduction and differential steering. 15 mph.
Arms: 2 pdr gun, 3 in howitzer, 1 machine gun. 5 crew.
Dimensions: 24 ft 5 in × 10 ft 8 in × 8 ft 2 in. 39 tons approx.

WW II (GB)

Mk 'Churchill' III (A22)

It appeared in 1942 with a 6 pdr gun replacing the 2 pdr of the earlier productions. The turret was a welded unit. 'Churchill' IV was the same except for a cast turret. Armour was 85 mm thick.
Type: Infantry tank.
Engine: Bedford Twin-Six, flat-12, 350 bhp at 2,200 rpm. Liquid.
Transmission: 4 F 1 R, epicyclic reduction and differential steering. 15 mph.
Arms: 6 pdr gun, 2 machine guns, 2 in bomb thrower. 5 crew.
Dimensions: 25 ft 2 in × 10 ft 8 in × 9 ft 2 in. 39 tons approx.

WW II (F)

ARL 44

This heavy tank was designed during 1944–5 and was also known as the *Char de Transition ARL44*. The co-producers were Renault and FAMH, under ARL (*Atelier de Rueil*) 'parentage'. Schneider and Simca produced the turrets and their traversing gear respectively. These tanks (60 were built) made only one public appearance, on 14 July 1951 (National Day Parade) and never saw active service.
Type: Heavy tank.
Engine: Maybach HL 230 P30, 12-in-V, 700 bhp at 3,000 rpm. Liquid.
Transmission: Manual gearbox with controlled differential steering. 40 kph.
Arms: 90 mm gun, 2–3 machine guns. 5 crew.
Dimensions: 10.52 m × 3.4 m × 3.2 m. 48 tons approx.

WW II (GB)
'Tortoise' (A39)

This huge vehicle, which had a cast one-piece superstructure, was designed by Nuffield Mechanizations and was entirely different from any other British tank of World War II. As it was, only six pilot vehicles were produced and they were not delivered until after the war. Armour was up to 9 in thick.
Type: Heavy tank.
Engine: Rolls-Royce Meteor, 12-in-V, 600–650 bhp at 2,500 rpm. Liquid.
Transmission: Merritt Brown 5 F 5 R, controlled differential steering. 12 mph, 4 mph cross country.
Arms: 32 pdr gun, 3 machine guns. 7 crew.
Dimensions: 33 ft (hull 23 ft 9 in) × 12 ft 10 in × 10 ft. 78 tons approx.

WW II (USA)

M6A1

Only a few M6 Series heavy tanks were produced, by Baldwin Locomotive Works, during 1942–4. These had various transmission systems and other detail variations. None saw active service.

Type: Heavy tank.

Engine: Wright Whirlwind G200, 9-radial, 775 bhp at 2,300 rpm. Air.

Transmission: Torque converter transmission, controlled differential steering with Budd Disk hydro-mechanical brakes. 25 mph.

Arms: 3 in gun, 37 mm gun, 4 machine guns, 1 sub-machine gun. 6 crew.

Dimensions: 300 in × 126 in × 124 in. 120,000 lbs approx.

WW II Škoda (ČS)

'Hetzer'/G13

The 'Hetzer' tank destroyer was produced during 1943–5 by Škoda for the German Army, but after the war 150 were supplied from war surplus stocks to Switzerland. The Swiss designated it G13 and later fitted a number with 8 cyl. Saurer diesel engines. One of these is shown.

Type: Self-propelled artillery.
Engine: Praga AC, 6-in-line, 160 bhp at 2,800 rpm. Liquid.
Transmission: Praga-Wilson pre-selector 5F 1 R planetary gearbox, clutch brake steering. 43 kph.
Arms: 7.5 cm gun, 1 machine gun. 4 crew.
Dimensions: 4.85 m (with gun 6.65 m) ×2.65 m×2.17 m. 16,000 kg approx.

WW II Büssing-NAG/Tatra (D)

3.7 cm Flak 43 auf sWS

The sWS (*schwere Wehrmacht-Schlepper*) superseded the 5 ton Sd.Kfz.6 semi-track vehicle in production in 1943. In addition to a soft-skin version with wooden cargo-body, there was the partly armoured model shown here and a full-armoured 10-barrel rocket launcher. They were produced by Büssing-NAG and Tatra.

Type: Self-propelled artillery.
Engine: Maybach HL 42TRKMS, 6-in-line, 100 bhp at 3,000 rpm. Liquid.
Transmission: 4 F 1 R with 2-speed auxiliary gear, front wheel and final drive disc brake steering. 25 kph.
Arms: 3.7 cm anti-aircraft gun. 2 crew.
Dimensions: 7 m×2.5 m×3.4 m (approx). 13,000 kg approx.

WW II (D)

'Jagdpanther'

The 'Jagdpanther' was derived from the 'Panther' heavy tank and was used chiefly as a tank destroyer. It was in production during the last two years of the war and the specimen shown is at the Royal Armoured Corps Tank Museum at Bovington, England.
Type: Self-propelled artillery.
Engine: Maybach HL230 P30, 12-in-V, 700 bhp at 3,000 rpm. Liquid.
Transmission: ZF-Synchron 7 F 1 R, controlled differential steering. 46 kph.
Arms: 8.8 cm anti-tank gun, 1 machine gun. 5 crew.
Dimensions: 9.86 m × 3.27 m × 2.72 m. 46,000 kg (gross).

WW II (GB)

3 in Mortar Carrier No. 1, Mks I & II

A variant of the infantry carrier. The mortar was stowed at the rear of the hull, over the axle.
Type: Self-propelled artillery.
Engine: Ford V8, 8-in-V, 65 bhp. Liquid.
Transmission: 4 F 1 R, steering-wheel operated moving cross tube, warping the tracks and brakes with differential for fast turns. 30 mph.
Arms: 3 in mortar. 5 crew.
Dimensions: 12 ft × 6 ft 9 in × 5 ft 3 in. $3\frac{3}{4}$–$4\frac{1}{4}$ tons.

WW II (GB)

A.A. Mks I & II

The four Besa anti-aircraft machine guns were mounted in a row in a special turret. The Mk II model was similar to the Mk I apart from modified sighting gear. They were based on the Tank, Light, Mk VI A and Mk VI B respectively. 1940.

Type: Self-propelled artillery.

Engine: Meadows, 6-in-line, 88.8 bhp. Liquid.

Transmission: 5 F 1 R, clutch steering and annular spur reduction. 32½ mph.

Arms: 4 7.92 mm machine guns.

Dimensions: 12 ft 11¼ in × 6 ft 8¾ in. 5 tons approx.

WW II (GB)

'Crusader' A.A. Mk I

A modification of the 'Crusader' Mk II cruiser tank. The open-top all-round gun shield was not fitted on early production models. 1943–4.
Type: Self-propelled artillery.
Engine: Nuffield Liberty, 12-in-V, 340 bhp at 1,500 rpm. Liquid.
Transmission: 4 F 1 R, Wilson epicyclic steering gear with skid brakes, pneumatically controlled. 27 mph.
Arms: 40 mm Bofors gun (anti-aircraft). 4 crew.
Dimensions: 20 ft 7½ in × 8 ft 8 in. 19 tons approx.

WW II (GB)
'Crusader' A.A. Mk II

A modification of the 'Crusader' Mk III cruiser tank. Armour thickness was 50–30 mm. The 'Crusader' A.A. Mk III was similar apart from the relocation of the radio equipment. 1944.
Type: Self-propelled artillery.
Engine: Nuffield Liberty, 12-in-V, 340 bhp at 1,500 rpm. Liquid.
Transmission: 4 F 1 R, Wilson epicyclic steering gear with skid brakes, pneumatically controlled. 27 mph, 15 mph cross country.
Arms: Twin 20 mm Oerlikon guns (anti-aircraft). 4 crew.
Dimensions: 20 ft 7½ in × 8 ft 8 in. 19 tons approx.

WW II Vickers (GB)
'Valentine', Mk I 'Archer'

Basically a 'Valentine' tank chassis with all-welded open-top superstructure, 665 were produced by Vickers in 1944. The gun was pointed to the rear. Armour was 8–60 mm thick.
Type: Self-propelled artillery.
Engine: General Motors 6–71M (2-stroke diesel), 6-in-line, 192 bhp at 1,900 rpm. Liquid.
Transmission: Skid steering by clutch and brake. 20 mph.
Arms: 17 pdr gun, 1 machine gun. 4 crew.
Dimensions: 21 ft 11 in×9 ft ½ in×7 ft 4½ in. 16 tons approx.

WW II (GB)
'Valentine', Mk I 'Bishop'

A modification of the 'Valentine' infantry tank, this vehicle was generally known as 'Bishop'. Armour thickness was 8–60 mm. They were used in North Africa with the Eighth Army and the First Army, but were not too successful.
Type: Self-propelled artillery.
Engine: AEC A190 (diesel), 6-in-line, 131–150 bhp. Liquid.
Transmission: Vickers double epicyclic reduction with steering clutches. 15 mph.
Arms: 25 pdr gun. 4 crew.
Dimensions: 18 ft 2 in×8 ft 7½ in×9 ft 1 in. 17.2 tons.

WW II (GB)

'Churchill' 3 in Gun, Mk I

A limited-production tank destroyer with 3 in AA gun in a limited-traverse mount on a 'Churchill' tank chassis. 1942.
Type: Self-propelled artillery.
Engine: Bedford Twin-Six, flat-12, 350 bhp at 2,200 rpm. Liquid.
Transmission: 4 F 1 R, epicyclic reduction and differential steering. 15 mph.
Arms: 3 in gun. 4 crew.
Dimensions: 26 ft 1 in × 10 ft 8 in × 9 ft 1 in. 39 tons approx.

WW II White (USA)

M4A1 Half-track

Made by the White Motor Co. as one of many variants in the US family of World War II half-tracks, other versions were produced also by Autocar and Diamond T. The basic vehicles were the M2 and the M3. The vehicle shown was based on the M2. Armour was 6.35 mm thick.

Type: Self-propelled artillery.

Engine: White 160AX, 6-in-line, 147 bhp at 3,000 rpm. Liquid.
Transmission: 4 F 1 R, 2-speed transfer case, front wheel steering. 45 mph.
Arms: 81 mm mortar, 1 machine gun (on track rail). 6 crew.
Dimensions: 244 in × 87½ in × 89 in (hull). 20,140 lbs (gross).

WW II Cadillac (USA)
M8

This was based on the M5 light tank (larger open-top turret) and produced by the Cadillac Division of General Motors from 1942 until 1944. It saw service in Italy and NW Europe, it also appeared with sand shields.
Type: Self-propelled artillery.
Engine: 2 Cadillac Series 42, 8-in-V (each), 125 bhp. Liquid.
Transmission: 2 Hydramatic automatic transmissions, 4 F 1 R, 2-speed transfer case, controlled differential steering. 36 mph.
Arms: 75 mm howitzer, 1 machine gun. 4 crew.
Dimensions: 196 in × 91½ in × 107 in. 34,570 lbs approx.

WW II Buick (USA)

M18 'Hellcat'

Over 2,500 of these tank destroyers were built by the Buick Division of General Motors during 1943–4. It was the fastest tracked AFV of the period, being capable of speeds up to 50 mph. Early models used the 350 bhp Continental R975C1 engine.

Type: Self-propelled artillery.
Engine: Continental R975C4, 9-radial, 400 bhp at 2,400 rpm. Air.
Transmission: Torqmatic 3 F 1 R automatic, controlled differential steering. 45–50 mph.
Arms: 76 mm gun, 1 machine gun.
5 crew.
Dimensions: 262 in × 113 in × 101 in.
38,910 lbs approx.

WW II (USA)
M36

Based on the M4 'Sherman' medium tank chassis, this variant was designed as a tank destroyer. It was developed from the similar-looking M10. The gun usually had a muzzle-brake. There was a number of variants of both the M10 and the M36.
Type: Self-propelled artillery.
Engine: Ford GAA, 8-in-V, 450 bhp at 2,600 rpm. Liquid.
Transmission: 5 F 1 R, controlled differential steering. 30 mph, 18 mph cross country.
Arms: 90 mm gun, 1 machine gun. 5 crew.
Dimensions: 235 in × 120 in × 125 in. 61,000 lbs approx.

WW II (GB)
Starting and Charging Mk II

It was used for 'slave starting' of tank engines in the field and for recharging batteries. It was a modification of the unarmoured Loyd Carrier.
Type: Self-propelled starting and charging equipment.
Engine: Ford V8, 8-in-V, 85 bhp at 3,800 rpm. Liquid.
Transmission: 4 F 1 R, Ford steering by brakes on front and and rear sprockets. 30 mph.
Dimensions: 13 ft 7 in × 6 ft 9½ in × 7 ft 6 in (reducible to 4 ft 8 in). 3½–4 tons.

WW II (GB)

Mechanical Cable Layer, Mk I

It was based on the unarmoured Loyd carrier. The picture is showing a three-quarter rear view. The engine was the popular Ford 30 hp V8, which was used for many automotive and other applications during World War II.

Type: Cable layer.

Engine: Ford V8, 8-in-V, 85 bhp at 3,800 rpm. Liquid.

Transmission: 4 F 1 R, Ford steering by brakes on front and rear sprockets.

30 mph.

Crew: 3

Dimensions: 13 ft 7 in × 7 ft 9 in × 7 ft 6 in. 4 tons approx.

WW II Zündapp (D)

Sd. Kfz. 303, 'Goliath'

In 1942 the Germans introduced a small, expendable, demolition vehicle (Sd.Kfz.302), propelled by two electric starter motors. It was superseded by a petrol-engined version, a surviving example of which is shown. It carried 100 kg of explosives and was produced mainly by Zündapp.
Type: Demolition vehicle.
Engine: Zündapp SZ7, 2 cyl., 12.5 bhp. Air.
Transmission: 4F, chain-drive, wire-guided. 11 kph.
Crew: None (remote control).
Dimensions: 1.63 m×0.91 m×0.62 m. 430 kg approx.

WW II Metropolitan-Vickers (GB)

'Beetle'

In 1940, Metropolitan-Vickers Electrical Co. Ltd developed a prototype for a small tracked vehicle, powered by storage batteries and driven by electric motors at up to 18 mph. It carried an explosive charge of 170 lbs. Telecontrol was achieved by a 500-yd cable, unreeled by the unmanned vehicle. Detonation was by impact or telecontrol, as desired. Some fifty were made, including amphibious variants, after approval from the War Office. Eventually the project was dropped because the usefulness of the vehicle after the first surprise was likely to be considerably lessened by the provision of fairly simple 'anti-Beetle' obstacles by the enemy. The Germans themselves, however, did employ a similar device, called 'Goliath' (q.v.).
Type: Demolition vehicle/mobile land mine.
Engine: Electric.
Transmission: Wire-controlled. 18 mph.
Crew: None (remote control).

WW II (GB)

'Valentine' II & III, 'Scorpion'

This was a 'Valentine' II or III tank fitted with a 'Scorpion' device. The effect of the device was to detonate anti-tank mines, provided these were not buried more than three inches below the ground surface. The vehicle could clear a path about 9½ feet wide and was operated by two Ford V8 engines mounted in the turret.

Type: Mine-clearing vehicle.
Engine: AEC A190 (diesel), 6-in-line, 131 bhp at 1,800 rpm. Liquid.
Transmission: 5 F 1 R, skid steering by clutch and brake. 15 mph.
Crew: 3.
Dimensions: 17 ft 9 in×8 ft 7½ in×7 ft 5½ in. 17 tons approx.

WW II (GB)

'Matilda/Baron' III A

During 1941–3, several prototypes were produced for a flail-type mine-clearing vehicle based on the 'Matilda' tank, this was the final version. It had three uses: (a) destroying mines over a path of about 10 ft wide, (b) cutting a path through wire entanglements and (c) cutting away ground obstructions, such as the faces of tank traps. The 'Baron' could destroy mines buried to a depth of four inches and the flail was operated by two Bedford truck engines and gearboxes with a special selector gear, mounted pannier fashion one on each side of the vehicle. See 'Matilda' Infantry Tank (q.v.).

Type: Mine-clearing vehicle.

WW II (GB)

Bridgelayer 'Churchill' III & IV

A conversion of 'Churchill' III or IV infantry tank which carried a Bridge, 30-ft, No. 2. The bridge is shown in almost half-way position. Time for one complete launching (or recovery) cycle was just over 1½ minutes.
Type: Bridging vehicle.
Engine: Bedford Twin-Six, flat-12, 350 bhp at 2,200 rpm. Liquid.
Transmission: 4 F 1 R, epicyclic reduction and differential steering. 15 mph, 10 mph cross country.
Dimensions: 37 ft 6 in (travelling position) × 10 ft 6½ in × 11 ft 1 in (travelling position). 4.8 tons (bridge only).

WW II (GB)

Bridgelayer 'Covenanter'

This was a conversion of the 'Covenanter' I or IV cruiser tank. The bridge was of the folding or 'scissors' type and was 34 ft long and 9½ ft wide. 1941.
Type: Bridging vehicle.
Engine: Meadows DAV, flat-12, 300 bhp. Liquid.
Transmission: 4 F 1 R, Wilson epicyclic 2-speed steering. 30 mph.

WW II (GB)

'Churchill Ark' Mk II

The name 'Ark' originated from Armoured Ramp Carrier. Such vehicles drove into the required position, e.g. a ditch or against a wall after which the ramps were dropped allowing following vehicles to cross immediately. There was no provision on the vehicle for rehoisting the ramps. The type shown was a conversion of the 'Churchill' III tank by the 8th Army in Italy and was known as the Italian Pattern, as opposed to the UK pattern which was fundamentally similar but had trackways over its tracks (on the Italian Pattern the top runs of the Ark's own tracks served as trackways).

Type: Bridging vehicle.

WW II (D)

2 ton 'Maultier'

For use in the very difficult terrain in Russia, the German Army introduced half-track conversions of standard 3 ton trucks as made by Ford, Magirus/Klöckner-Deutz (shown) and Opel. The rear bogie suspension was of the British Carden-Loyd design.
Type: Half-track truck.
Engine: Deutz F4M513, 4-in-line, 80 bhp at 2,250 rpm. Liquid.
Transmission: 5 F 1 R (overdrive top), steering by front wheels and mechanical brakes on final drives. 28 kph.
Crew: 2.
Dimensions: 6.12 m × 2.22 m × 2.8 m. 4.650 kg approx.

WW II Diamond T (USA)
T16

A pilot model produced by Diamond T Motor Car Co in 1943. Other armoured half-track truck pilot models were made by Autocar, Mack and White but none reached quantity production stage.
Type: Half-track truck.
Engine: Hercules RXLD, 6-in-line, 174 bhp at 2,600 rpm. Liquid.
Transmission: Spicer automatic with torque converter, front wheel and controlled differential steering. 35 mph.
Crew: 14.
Dimensions: 247 in × 94 in × 94 in. 30,010 lbs (combat loaded).

WW II International (USA/GB)
Multiple gun M14/REME Fitters

Produced by International Harvester, 1600 of these AA gun carriages were supplied to the UK. The British removed the guns and converted the vehicles for other duties, including REME Fitters trucks for tank repairs in the field. An 'A'-frame at front was employed for lifting engines and other heavy components.
Type: Self-propelled artillery/mobile repair unit.
Engine: International Red Diamond RED450B, 6-in-line, 143 bhp at 2,600 rpm. Liquid.
Transmission: 4 F 1 R, 2-speed transfer case, front wheel steering. 45 mph.
Crew: 2+.
Dimensions: 20 ft 10 in × 7 ft 3 in × 7 ft 11 in. 17,024 lbs approx.

WW II (USA)
M32B1

Converted from M4A1 medium tank, the original turret was replaced by a fixed one and a 30 ton winch was added in the fighting compartment. It was used for the recovery of disabled tanks, etc., from the battlefield and also to provide a hoist for the removal of tank engines, turrets and final drives.
Type: Tank recovery vehicle.
Engine: Continental R975, 9-radial, 350–400 bhp at 2,400 rpm. Air.
Transmission: 5 F 1 R, controlled differential steering. 25 mph, 18 mph cross country.
Arms: 81 mm gun, 2 machine guns. 5 crew.
Dimensions: 322 in × 107 in × 252 in (reducible to 117 in). 61,700 lbs approx.

WW II (USA)
T33

Based on the M4A3E2 medium tank with horizontal volute spring suspension, it had a special turret. The flame fuel and propellant gas was carried inside the vehicle. It was an experimental model only (mid-1945).
Type: Flamethrower.
Engine: Ford GAA, 8-in-V, 450 bhp at 2,600 rpm. Liquid.
Transmission: 5 F 1 R, controlled differential steering. 26 mph, 15 mph cross country.
Arms: 75 mm anti-aircraft gun, co-axial flame projector. 5 crew.
Dimensions: 247 in × 112 in × 135 in. 84,000 lbs approx.

WW II (USA)
T1E3

Many special purpose vehicles were based on the ubiquitous 'Sherman' medium tank. Most of them were conversions rather than purpose-built vehicles; among these variants were bridging vehicles, rocket launchers, etc. Illustrated here is one of a range of mine-clearing devices. It was developed in 1943 and nicknamed 'Aunt Jemima'. It had two chain-driven roller units of 10 ft diameter steel discs and was used in Italy and Normandy in 1944.
Type: Mine-clearing vehicle.

1950s Pontiac (USA)
M76 'Otter'

Originally known as T46E1, it was produced by the Pontiac Division of General Motors. It is shown climbing over a rice paddy dike while delivering supplies to forward units of the 9th Marines in Vietnam, February 1967.
Type: Amphibian.
Engine: Continental A0268, flat-4 (vertically mounted), 127 bhp at 3,200 rpm. Air.
Transmission: Cross-drive with torque converter, hand-lever hydraulic, multi-disc steering brakes. 28 mph, 4 mph in water.
Arms: 1 machine gun. 2 crew.
Dimensions: 188 in × 98 in × 108 in (with propeller in water position). 12,165 lbs.

1950s (USA)
M41 'Walker Bulldog'

Basically a light tank but with the gun usually found on medium types, it was introduced in 1950 and known originally as the T41E1.
Type: Light tank.
Engine: Continental AOS895–3, flat-6, 500 bhp at 2,800 rpm. Air.
Transmission: Cross-drive with torque converter, hand-lever controlled, multi-disc steering brakes. 40 mph.
Arms: 76 mm gun, 2 machine guns. 4 crew.
Dimensions: 317 in × 128 in × 111 in. 51,000 lbs approx.

1950s (GB)

'Centurion' Mk 5

First introduced just before the end of the war, the 'Centurion' was produced in large quantities and many variants until the 1960s. The Mk 5 first appeared in late 1952 under the design parentage of Vickers-Armstrong. The one shown is minus the usual side plates and with the gun in the travelling crutch on the rear deck.
Type: Medium tank.

Engine: Rolls-Royce Meteor Mk 4B, 12-in-V, 650 bhp at 2,550 rpm. Liquid.
Transmission: 5 F 2 R Merritt Brown, controlled differential steering. 22 mph.
Arms: 20 pdr gun, 2 machine guns. 4 crew.
Dimensions: 28 ft 3 in (32 ft 3 in with gun forward) × 11 ft 1 in (with side plates fitted) × 9 ft 8 in. 112,000 lbs approx.

1950s (USA)
M47 'Patton'

Although originally equipped with a 90 mm gun (1950), the tank shown is a French modification of the late 1960s, featuring a French 105 mm gun, firing the shell cartridges used in the 105 mm Mk F1 gun of the AMX30 tank.
Type: Medium tank.
Engine: Continental AV1790–5B, 12-in-V, 810 bhp at 2,800 rpm. Air.
Transmission: GM Allison cross-drive 2 F 1 R, combining torque converter and steering mechanism. 37 mph.
Arms: 90 mm gun, 3 machine guns. 5 crew.
Dimensions: 334 in × 139 in × 118 in. 97,200 lbs approx.

1950s (USA)
M42

A self-propelled anti-aircraft weapon, introduced in 1953. It is shown here in service with the Japanese Self Defence Forces in the 1960s.
Type: Self-propelled artillery.
Engine: Continental AOS895–3, flat-6, 500 bhp at 2,800 rpm. Air.
Transmission: GM Allison cross-drive 2F1R combining torque converter. 45 mph.
Arms: Twin 40 mm guns, 1 machine gun. 6 crew.
Dimensions: 244 in×129 in×112 in. 43,000 lbs approx.

1950s (USA)
M53

This US Marine Corps photograph shows a unit of the First 155 Gun Battery firing on enemy-suspected positions at Phu Bai, Vietnam, in support of infantry troops on 7 February 1967. It was also available with an 8 in howitzer and was designated M5S.
Type: Self-propelled artillery.
Engine: Continental AV1790–5, 12-in-V, 704 bhp at 2,800 rpm. Air.
Transmission: GM cross-drive 2 F 1 R. 30 mph.
Arms: 155 mm gun, 1 machine gun. 6 crew.
Dimensions: 402 in × 140 in × 140 in. 96,000 lbs approx.

1950s (USSR)
ASU–57

A special lightweight SP assault gun, introduced about 1957. A heavier version, with more powerful six-cylinder engine (ZIL–123), also appeared. ASU in vehicle designation stands for *Aviadezantnaya Samochodnaya Ustanovska*, meaning airborne self-propelled mounting. It was supplied to several Warsaw Pact countries.
Type: Self-propelled artillery.
Engine: GAZ M20E, 4-in-line, 55 bhp. Liquid.
Transmission: 4 F 1 R, clutch and brake steering. 45 kph.
Arms: 57 mm anti-tank gun. 3 crew.
Dimensions: 3.48 m × 2.1 m × 1.2 m. 3.35 tons approx.

1950s (USSR)
ZSU–57–2

Introduced about 1957, tnis vehicle was based on the T54 tank chassis. The suspension of the T54 was modified (road wheels reduced from 5 to 4 and respaced). The letters ZSU in the vehicle designation stand for *Zenitnaya Samochodnaya Ustanovska*, meaning anti-aircraft self-propelled mounting.
Type: Self-propelled artillery.
Engine: V–2/54 (diesel), 12-in-V, 520 bhp at 2,000 rpm. Liquid.
Transmission: 5 F 1 R, clutch and brake steering. 48 kph.
Arms: Twin 57 mm anti-aircraft guns. 6 crew.
Dimensions: 6.22 m × 3.27 m × 2.75 m. 28 tons approx.

See following page

09

1950s (USSR)
FROG–1

A short-range missile transporter/launcher based on a Joseph Stalin (IS) tank chassis. FROG stands for Free Rocket Over Ground. It made its public debut at the 7 November 1957 parade in Moscow.
Type: Rocket launcher.
Engine: V-2-1S, 12-in-V (diesel), 513 bhp at 2,000 rpm. Liquid.
Transmission: 4 F 1 R, 2-stage regenerative steering system. 37 kph.
Arms: 3,175 kg unguided field artillery rocket, 10.2 m long, 32 km range.
4 crew.
Dimensions: 10.7 m (including rocket) ×3.2 m×3.32 m (including rocket).
36.5 tons approx. including rocket.

1950s (GB)
'Centurion' Mk 2

Developed in the early 1950s by the Fighting Vehicles Research and Development Establishment (now MVEE) as ARV FV4006, it is based on the 'Centurion' Mk 3. It has an electric winch for a 30 ton single line pull, powered by a 160 bhp Rolls-Royce B80 petrol engine. It is also available with a 10 ton lift jib and rear spade. It is shown in use with the Australian Army.
Type: Recovery vehicle.

Engine: Rolls-Royce Meteor, 12-in-V, 650 bhp at 2,550 rpm. Liquid.
Transmission: 5F2R Merritt Brown, controlled differential steering. 22 mph.
Arms: 1 machine gun, smoke dischargers. 3–4 crew.
Dimensions: 29 ft 5 in (including spade) × 11 ft $1\frac{1}{2}$ in × 9 ft 6 in. 111,000 lbs approx.

1950s Vickers-Armstrong (GB)

Vickers 'Vigor'

A commercial-type tractor produced by Vickers-Armstrong (Tractors) Ltd during the late 1950s. The vehicle shown was one of several still in service with the British Army in the early 1970s. Weight and dimensions listed below are exclusive of the blade and associated equipment.
Type: Bulldozer.
Engine: Rolls-Royce C6SFL (diesel, supercharged), 6-in-line, 180 bhp. Liquid.
Transmission: 6 F 3 R (or Rolls-Royce torque converter with 3-speed gearbox), controlled differential steering. 6 mph.
Crew: 1.
Dimensions: 14 ft $8\frac{1}{2}$ in × 8 ft 6 in × 9 ft 11 in. 36,000 lbs approx.

1960s (USSR)
ATS–59

Introduced in 1959, this Soviet medium artillery tractor replaced the earlier AT–S and is used as a prime mover for 130 mm field gun, 152 mm gun-howitzer, 100 mm AA gun and other artillery pieces. The engine is located behind the cab. Its towed load is 14,000 kg.

Type: Artillery tractor.
Engine: A–650 (diesel), 12-in-V, 300 bhp. Liquid.
Transmission: Controlled differential steering. 40 kph.
Crew: 2+14.
Dimensions: 6.3 m × 2.8 m × 2.5 m. 16,000 kg approx.

1960s Volvo (S)
BV202E

An articulated amphibious over-snow carrier, produced by Bolinder-Munktell (Volvo) and supplied to the armies of Sweden, Norway, Great Britain (as shown). It is also known as 'Snowcat'.
Type: Amphibian.
Engine: Volvo B18, 4-in-line, 91 bhp at 5,300 rpm. Liquid.
Transmission: 4 F 1 R with 2-speed transfer case, controlled articulation of front and rear unit to steer. 40 kph, 1.25 knots in water.
Crew: 2.
Dimensions: 6.17 m × 1.76 m × 2.21 m. 3,200 kg approx.

1960s (USA)
M116 'Husky'

An air-transportable light-weight carrier, designed in the late 1950s to replace the earlier 'Weasel' and 'Otter' amphibians. This is a prototype, photographed at McChord Air Force Base, Washington, in November 1958.
Type: Amphibian.
Engine: Chevrolet 283 CID, 8-in-V, 160 bhp at 4,600 rpm. Liquid.
Transmission: Hydramatic automatic, controlled differential steering. 32 mph, 4 mph in water.
Arms: 1 machine gun. 1+13 crew.
Dimensions: 188 in × 82 in × 79 in (reducible to 64 in). 7,880 lbs approx.

1960s (USSR)
Full-track PTS–M

The PTS–M amphibian was introduced in the late 1960s and is used for ferrying of vehicles, weapons and equipment up to 10 tons, or up to 70 troops. On land the payload is 5 tons.
Type: Amphibian.
Engine: Diesel, 6-in-line, 180 bhp. Liquid.
Transmission: Controlled planetary differential steering, 2 propellers. 40 kph, 15 kph in water.
Crew: 2.
Dimensions: 11.5 m × 3.3 m × 2.65 m. 17,700 kg approx.

1960s (ČS)
OT–62 'TOPAS'

A Czechoslovakian version of the Soviet BTR–50PK, used by the Czech and Polish (as shown) armed forces. It was based on the Soviet PT–76 light amphibious tank. There were also several derivations, including an armoured ambulance.
Type: Armoured personnel carrier.

Engine: PV–6 (diesel), 6-in-line, 300 bhp. Liquid.
Transmission: 5 F 1 R, clutch and brake steering. 62 kph, 11 kph in water.
Crew: 2+18.
Dimensions: 7.08 m × 3.14 m × 2.1 m. 15 tons approx.

1960s (USA)
M113

Widely used by several nations in standard and special versions, the M113A1 has a GM V6 diesel engine. It is shown with a rolling liquid transporter in May 1960. A 0.50 calibre machine gun may be fitted on a pintle mount on the commander's cupola.
Type: Armoured personnel carrier.

Engine: Chrysler 75M, 8-in-V, 215 bhp at 4,000 rpm. Liquid.
Transmission: GM Allison TX200 automatic with differential band and disc brakes. 40 mph.
Crew: 2+11.
Dimensions: 191½ in × 106 in × 79 in. 22,615 lbs approx.

1960s Vickers (GB)
MBT Mk I

This Main Battle Tank was designed by Vickers Ltd to meet the needs of those countries which desire a tank in the 35–40 ton class. It is produced both by Vickers and by the Indian Government in a special factory in Madras, both for the Indian Army.
Type: Battle tank.
Engine: Leyland L60 (multi-fuel), 6-cyl. with 12 opposed pistons, 650 bhp at 2,670 rpm. Liquid.
Transmission: TN12 gearbox combining Wilson epicyclic gear-change with Merritt steering system, 6 F 2 R. 35 mph.
Arms: 105 mm gun, 2 machine guns. 4 crew.
Dimensions: 32 ft 1 in (gun forward) ×10 ft 5 in×8 ft. 85,000 lbs (loaded).

1960s (J)
Type 61/STA–4

Development work on this, the first post-war Japanese tank, started in 1954–5 and after trials with a series of prototypes during the late 1950s and early 1960s, quantity production commenced in 1962. It is a conventional design, with a strong American influence.
Type: Battle tank.
Engine: Mitsubishi 12HM (diesel, supercharged), 12-in-V, 600 bhp at 2,100 rpm. Air.
Transmission: Controlled differential steering. 45 kph.
Arms: 90 mm gun, 2 machine guns. 4 crew.
Dimensions: 6.3 m × 2.95 m × 2.48 m. 35,000 kg approx.

1960s (S)

Strv 103, 'S'-tank

Developed during the late 1950s and early 1960s the Bofors 'S'-tank is unusual in that its gun is rigidly mounted in the hull, gun-laying being achieved by traversing or altering the pitch of the whole vehicle. The first production models were delivered in 1967. It is fitted with a bulldozer blade to dig its own protective emplacement.
Type: Battle tank.
Engine: FN-Boeing 553 gas turbine and Rolls-Royce K60 diesel, (RR) 6 with 12 pistons, (FN–B) 490 bhp (RR) 240 bhp. (RR) liquid.
Transmission: Volvo-Matic hydraulic torque converter, controlled differential steering. 50 kph.
Arms: 105 mm gun, 4 machine guns. 3 crew.
Dimensions: 8.8 m×3.3 m×1.9 m. 37,000 kg approx.

1960s (USA)
M60A1

An improved edition of the M60 of the late 1950s, which, in turn, was developed from the M48 medium tank of 1954 (and its developments). The M60A1 entered production in October 1962 and, in improved form, will remain in use well into the 1970s.

Type: Battle tank.
Engine: Continental AVDS 1790–2A (diesel), 12-in-V, 750 bhp at 2,400 rpm. Air.
Transmission: GM Allison cross-drive, combines gearbox, differential, steering and braking units. 30 mph.
Arms: 105 mm gun, 2 machine guns. 4 crew.
Dimensions: 366 in × 143 in × 128 in. 106,000 lbs approx.

1960s Vickers (GB)
'Abbot' FV433

The 'Abbot' is based on the chassis of the FV432 APC. It went into production by Vickers in the mid-1960s and is in service with the Royal Artillery both at home and in Germany (BAOR). The vehicle features a built-in flotation screen, permitting deep water, river and estuary crossings.
Type: Self-propelled artillery.

Engine: Rolls-Royce K60 (multi-fuel), 6 with 12 pistons opposed, 240 bhp at 3,750 rpm. Liquid.
Transmission: Automatic, controlled differential steering. 30 mph.
Arms: 105 mm gun, 1 machine gun. 4 crew.
Dimensions: 19 ft 2 in × 8 ft 8 in × 8 ft 2 in. 38,500 lbs (loaded).

1960s (USSR)
ASU–85

A highly mobile, air-transportable SP assault gun, particularly suitable as a tank destroyer, by day and night. Based on the chassis of the PT–76 light amphibious tank, the ASU–85 was introduced about 1962 to supersede the earlier ASU–57 (q.v.).
Type: Self-propelling artillery.
Engine: T–54V–2 (diesel), 6-in-V, 240 bhp at 1,200 rpm. Liquid.
Transmission: 5 F 1 R, clutch and brake steering. 45 kph.
Arms: 85 mm anti-tank gun, 1 machine gun. 4 crew.
Dimensions: 6 m (without gun) × 2.8 m × 2.1 m. 14 tons approx.

1960s (D)
'Leopard'

The standard tank of German *Bundeswehr* and several other NATO countries, this *Kampfpanzer* was based on a design by Porsche and produced by a consortium of German firms. Final assembly is by Krauss-Maffei, the main contractors. Developed during the early 1960s, over 2,000 had been delivered by 1970.
Type: Battle tank.
Engine: Daimler-Benz MB838 (multi-fuel), 10-in-V, 830 bhp at 2,200 rpm. Liquid.
Transmission: ZF four-speed planetary with hydraulic torque converter. 65 kph.
Arms: 105 mm gun, 2 machine guns. 4 crew.
Dimensions: 9.54 m (gun forward) × 3.25 m × 2.38 m. 40,000 kg approx.

1960s (F)
Poseur de Pont

The scissors-type Class 25 Mk F1 38 ft-span bridging equipment by Ets. Coder on the chassis of the AMX13 light tank. Also available with Mk F1A span, two of which locked together being suitable for crossing of Class 50 equipment. This is one of several special-purpose vehicles based on the famed AMX13 which was introduced in 1951 and became one of the world's best AFVs.

Type: Bridging vehicle.
Engine: SAVIEM/SOFAM 8Gxb, flat-8, 250–270 bhp at 3,200 rpm. Liquid.
Transmission: 5 F 1 R, controlled differential steering. 40 kph.
Crew: 3.
Dimensions: 8.02 m×3.16 m×4.05 m. 19,200 kg approx.

1960s Caterpillar (USA/GB)
Caterpillar D6C

Introduced in 1963, the Caterpillar D6C is a commercial-type medium-size full-track tractor with angling bulldozer, i.e. the dozer blade may be used 25° to either side or straight.
Type: Bulldozer.
Engine: Caterpillar D6 (diesel), 6-in-line, 125 bhp. Liquid.
Transmission: 5 F 4 R, planetary 'Power Shift' transmission, hydraulically actuated steering clutches. 5.9 mph.
Crew: 1.
Dimensions: 16 ft 3 in×10 ft×8 ft 10 in (exhaust stack). 29,000 lbs approx.

1970s (F)
AMX10P

The 1971 prototype is shown. The 1969 prototype was presented as the AMX10A amphibious infantry combat vehicle. AMX10R was basically the same vehicle but wheeled (6×6) instead of tracked.
Type: Armoured personnel carrier.
Engine: SAVIEM/Hispano-Suiza HS115 (diesel), 8-in-V, 275 bhp at 3,000 rpm. Liquid.
Transmission: Hydraulic torque converter with manual 4 F 1 R gearbox (water propulsion by hydrojet, tracks or a combination of both). 65 kph.
Arms: 20 mm gun, 1 machine gun. 2+9 crew.
Dimensions: 5.85 m×2.78 m×2.5 m. 12,500 kg approx.

1970s Alvis (GB)
'Scorpion' FV101

The 'Scorpion' is the Fire Support Vehicle of the Alvis CVR(T) range of vehicles (Combat Vehicle, Reconnaissance [Tracked]). It has aluminium alloy armour and swimming capability. Derivatives include an APC, a command vehicle, an ambulance, etc.
Type: Light tank.
Engine: Jaguar XK 4.2 litre, 6-in-line, 195 bhp at 5,000 rpm. Liquid.
Transmission: Cross-drive semi-automatic hot-shift, 7 F 7 R, pivot turn. 54 mph.
Arms: 76 mm gun, 1 machine gun. 3 crew.
Dimensions: 14 ft 5 in × 7 ft 2 in × 6 ft 11 in. 17,500 lbs (loaded).

1970s Hägglund (S)
Infanterikanonvagn 91

The ikv 91 is a light amphibious tank designed by AB Hägglund & Söner as the main contractors to the Material Administration of the Swedish Armed Forces. Its main role is that of a tank destroyer.
Type: Light tank.
Engine: Volvo-Penta (turbo-charged diesel), 6-in-line, 330 bhp at 2,200 rpm. Liquid.
Transmission: Volvo-Penta 8 F 2 R, clutch and brake steering (Hydrostatic system available). 67 kph, 8 kph in water.
Arms: 90 mm gun, 2 machine guns. 4 crew.
Dimensions: 8.74 m × 3 m × 2.41 m. 15,000 kg approx.

1970s (GB)
'Chieftain' Mk 3 FV4201

Britain's current main battle tank was under development throughout the 1960s. In 1965–6, batches of Mk 1 and 2 models were issued to the British Army. The Mk 3 was introduced in September 1969. Variants include an ARV (armoured recovery vehicle) and a bridging vehicle. Photo (British Official) shows a Chieftain of 17/21st Lancers at Sennelager, Germany.
Type: Main battle tank.
Engine: Leyland L60 (multi-fuel), 6-cyl. with 12 opposed pistons, 650 bhp at 2,100 rpm (Mk 5: 840 bhp). Liquid.
Transmission: Merritt Wilson TN12 6 F 2 R, Merritt regenerative steering with hydraulic disc brakes. 25 mph.
Arms: 120 mm gun, 3 machine guns. 4 crew.
Dimensions: 35 ft 9 in × 11 ft 6 in × 9 ft 6 in. 53 tons approx.

See following page

03 EB 35

1970s (GB)
'Swingfire' FV438

One of the several variants of the FV432 APC (armoured personnel carrier), which was introduced during the 1960s. This version launches wire-guided missiles, loaded and operated from within the vehicle. Additional missiles are carried in the vehicle, which can swim from ship to shore with the built-in flotation screen erected.

Type: Missile launcher.
Engine: Rolls-Royce K60 (multi-fuel), 6-cyl. with 12 opposed pistons, 240 bhp at 3,750 rpm. Liquid.
Transmission: Automatic, controlled differential steering. 32.5 mph, $3\frac{1}{4}$–4 knots in water.
Arms: 2 BAC 'Swingfire' anti-tank missiles, 1 machine gun. 2 crew.
Dimensions: 16 ft 9 in×9 ft 9 in×8 ft $10\frac{1}{2}$ in. 35,000 lbs (loaded).

1970s (F)
Systeme Pluton

The Pluton surface-to-surface tactical weapon system was introduced in prototype form in 1971 and is based on the chassis of the AMX30 medium tank. The missile consists of a nuclear warhead incorporating firing devices and a body comprising a guidance compartment, a solid-propellent rocket motor stage and a cross-shaped fin.
Type: Missile launcher.
Engine: SAVIEM/Hispano-Suiza HS110 (multi-fuel), flat–12, 720 bhp at 2,400 rpm. Liquid.
Transmission: Centrifugal automatic clutch, 5 F 1 R mechanical gearbox, controlled differential steering. 60 kph.
Crew: 4.
Dimensions: Missile 7.6 m long, vehicle 3.1 m wide. Missile weighs 2,400 kg.

Index